CONTENTS

MEGALITHS
STONES OF MEMORY

Jean-Pierre Mohen

DISCOVERIES®
HARRY N. ABRAMS, INC., PUBLISHERS

Menhirs, dolmens, cromlechs: these are the names of legend. Scholars know them as standing stones, burial chambers, and stone circles. Such megaliths stood for seven thousand years along the western edge of Europe, from Portugal to Scandinavia, practically forming a wall against the Atlantic, before their massive presence and the persistent myths surrounding them seized the world's imagination.

CHAPTER 1
THE STONES OF LEGEND

The inspiration of legend and the site of ceremony, megaliths are at the heart of the European imagination. Stonehenge (right) is depicted as a center of Druidic rites. At Quiberon (opposite) in Brittany, the menhirs of Le Moulin provided the setting for bonfires on St. John's Day.

Stones—heathen and biblical

In 398 AD in Carthage, and again in
452 (Arles), 567 (Tours), 681 (Toledo),
and 826 (Paris), Church councils
and synods denounced
standing stones and

In 1858 the French
novelist George Sand
devoted a story to the
megaliths in the region of
Berry. Her son, Maurice
Sand, illustrated them as
huge, intriguing heads
made of rough stone.
Sand wrote: "Sometimes

specifically condemned
their worship.

In that era of ascendant Christianity, such persistent
resolve reflects the tenacity of the mysterious faiths in
which the megaliths played a part. Fear of the huge
stones led to some of them being destroyed. St. Eloi
became the shatterer of these pagan idols. But popular
beliefs are deep-seated and secretive; it is impossible
to obliterate their mark entirely. They give birth to
enigmatic place names that conjure up images of fairies,
dwarfs, giants, and devils, sometimes even local saints. In
the 18th century antiquarians consulted the Bible as the
ancient, primary reference. They found that Moses
himself had ordered the use of stone altars untouched by
steel, "For if thou lift up thy tool upon it, thou hast
polluted it." The discovery of polished-stone axes right
next to some megaliths seemed to prove that the stones
were the altars Moses had demanded.

we have seen these so-
called loose stones or silly
stones with their many
irregular holes that give
them the look of mon-
strous faces. Road inspec-
tors, happening on them,
had them destroyed,
which is no more than
they deserved."

Gargantua's finger, Pantagruel's table

In the fifth chapter of *Pantagruel* (1532), French author
François Rabelais tells how the hero, a giant, wanted to
have a banquet table for his student friends and took a

The giant Pantagruel
put up the Raised
Stone of Poitiers, a
huge banquet table for
students, who would be
more eager to fill their
stomachs than their
minds. A 16th-century
engraving (opposite,
below) depicts the
dolmen in which the
names of university
professors are carved.

huge rock some 25 yards around (23 meters) "and placed it firmly on four pillars at the center of a field; so that those same scholars, at such times when they knew of naught else to do, could pass their time by climbing onto this very stone and feasting there, with flagons, hams, and pies, and mark their names upon it, and now it is known as the Raised Stone." This was a lighthearted way of talking about a monument from the "postdiluvian" (post-Flood) age—the cautious language of the time employed the biblical allusion to offset any dangerous reference to the "pagan" stones, whose worship had been proscribed by the Church. By referring to the legendary Pantagruel, Rabelais incorporated the megalith into a French tradition, and the monument erected by the giant was thus stripped of any negative aura—though not of its magic origin. Many French megaliths evoke the mythical time of the Giants. Two menhirs are attributed to Pantagruel's father, Gargantua: his "Tooth" at St.-Suliac and his "Finger" at Fort La Latte. Petrified giants and ogres share in the very beginnings of the standing stones.

In his *Historia* of 1567, Olaus Magnus depicts the megaliths of Sweden and Norway as geometric steles forming a forest of gravestones that giants had constructed for soldiers' tombs (above).

Legends of fairies, sibyls, Medusa

La Roche aux Fées (Fairies' Rock) at Essé, France, is composed of red shale blocks that fairies are said to have carried in their aprons from an outcropping 3 miles (4 km) away. The menhir of Rumfort is one of the rocks that were dropped along the way. According to the Arthurian myth, the tomb of Merlin the Magician is in Brocéliande woods, where a megalithic coffer shelters the fairy Vivian. As late as 1660 the Sybil of Drenthe, Holland, held court beneath a dolmen, still proffering her oracular visions. In Corsica the stories behind most of the anthropomorphic (human-shaped) menhirs attest to the presence of Medusa, who turned all who glanced at her to stone. Another legend relates to Néant-sur-Yvel, France, where St. Méen turned debauched monks to stone; and the famous alignments (long rows of menhirs) of Carnac are what remains of the three thousand legionnaires petrified by God as they pursued St. Cornelius. At Langon and St.-Just, France, the megaliths are the Petrified Maidens, punished for having danced

Megaliths served as scenery for the witches' sabbath (above and opposite, above). It was also said that the stones at Carnac came to drink on Christmas night at St.-Colomban (below).

near the coast at vespers, and the same fate befell a priest in Bristol, England, who failed to say mass.

Erected by supernatural forces, some stones are often shaken by mysterious seizures. The menhir of St. Martin-d'Arcé rotates at the stroke of midnight, while that at Culey-le-Patry moves only to the sound of the cock's crow. Others twirl during midnight mass on Christmas or, as at Mesnil-Hardray, rise, making way for a procession of white-clad maidens who come to dance in a circle on the Landes. At Carnac the stones take themselves down to the sea for a swim; and once in a hundred years, at exactly midnight on Christmas, the menhirs of Plouhinec appear at the river to take a drink. There is a hex on anyone who dares question these "facts." The stones were felt to contain living beings, unseen but real, genial yet easily offended.

Stones as guardians of health

It is said that megaliths can work white magic. The huge phallic monuments promote love, fertility, and health. Many legends and practices connected to dolmens and menhirs are concerned with male virility and female fertility. In France young women would pull up their skirts to straddle the Pierre-de-Chantecoq or the pillar of La Roche-Marie, and they would slide, legs astride, down the leaning menhir of La Tremblais at St.-Samson-sur-Rance. To assure themselves beautiful progeny, husbands and wives would rub their naked bellies along the two sides of the menhir of Kerloas at Plouarzel, and at Nohant-Vic, barren

women were advised to suck on a chip of red sandstone taken from the slab of a dolmen.

Similarly, slabs with holes were known to confer virility. The one named for Constantine in Cornwall, England, was used to purify infants; parents passed babies through the hole in a symbolic rebirth to ensure good health. The "hole of the soul" in the megalithic graves in the Paris basin was said to be able to resuscitate the spirit of the departed as it entered and left the tomb. Even the passageways of these graves, often completely blocked by stones, had their own role as the symbolic channel for messages that could revitalize the living and the dead.

The Christianization of the megaliths

Old beliefs die hard. The Church, though no friend of such superstitions, knew better than to confront them head on and eventually appropriated megalithic magic for itself. The Theodosian Code of the year 438 decreed that the Christian faith adapt its observances to pagan holy sites whose original rites, many of them very old, had been distorted, subdued, or largely obliterated by that time. A 16th-century painting in the Church of St.-Merry in Paris

Popular tradition often imbued the megaliths with a life force that would foster love and health. Such beliefs were reinforced by the phallic shape of many of the stones like the menhir of La Tremblais, France (opposite, above) which inspired circle dances, embraces, and rituals.

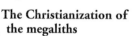

The women's circle at Plonéour-Lanvern (Brittany) in about 1900 (center), was unequivocally seen as a nuptial and fertility rite. The balanced slab called the Pierre aux Maris (Husbands' Stone) at La Baroche, Alsace (above, left), was visited by women seeking a spouse. The answer a prospective bride received depended on how much she could make the stone move. The health of newborn infants was said to be improved if they were passed through the hole in a slab megalith (above, the dolmen of Trie-Château).

depicts Ste. Geneviève, the city's protectress, surrounded by her sheep within a circle of standing stones overlooking the fortified city she has just rescued. Sometimes crosses were carved into or affixed to the megaliths' summits, such as at St.-Duzec, where the menhir was carved on one side with long folds reminiscent of a cape. It bore signs of the Passion on the other side and was topped with a cross. Eventually, some of the stone idols were silenced entirely. In one of the first official documents of St.-Cado, Brittany, dating from the year 1000, the megaliths were reduced to simple boundary markers, signposts for a reserved, hard-working people.

Ste. Geneviève, the patron saint of Paris, who protected the city from Attila's troops in the 5th century, sits symbolically surrounded by her sheep and a wall—in fact, a circle of standing stones. The picture displays the religious symbolism of the guardian circle as well as the conflation of Christianity with paganism.

Naming the stones

Documentation about the megaliths, which in Europe dates to the 16th century, suggests that the people who had daily contact with them were eager to explain their meaning. Only relatively recently, though—at the end of the 18th century—did the Bretons give the megaliths generic names. Standing stones were assigned the Celtic word *peulvan* and, more commonly, *menhir*. Enthusiasts of Celtic culture called stone circles, which were thought to work magic, by the Gallic name *cromlech*. The circle in the Brocéliande woods, for example, where the fairy Vivian had locked up her lover Merlin, was supposed to be able to make him invisible. In 1792 Théophile de La Tour d'Auvergne, a Breton soldier fascinated by ancient history, gave the tables where giants were said to feast a local Celtic name: "the huge stone covering this ancient monument is called, in our language, *dolmin*" (or *dolmen*, meaning "table"). The same stones were known in Germanic lands as *Hünenbedden* (chickens' beds) or *Riesengrabern* (giants' tombs). Unable to judge just how ancient the megaliths were, each culture that encountered them gave them names derived from its own roots. *Cairn* is borrowed from a Breton word for the mound of stones covering a megalithic tomb. Thus *Carnac* is

Two figures kneel in prayer at a menhir, St.-Duzec, at Plomeur (Côtes-d'Armor). A cross has been added on top, and the stone itself bears a painting of the Passion of Christ. The instruments and emblems of the sacrifice of the son of God are above the crucifixion. The pagan religious fervor once inspired by this enormous standing stone has become Christian. This is just one example of a Christianized monolith.

derived from the cairn that overlooks the town, the grave mound of St.-Michel.

The two major types of megalithic structures are classified as tombs (or "closed" architecture) and standing stones (or "open" architecture). But the two kinds are not necessarily unrelated: the "closed" structures were in fact open to their surrounding space; and offerings were placed at the base of the standing stones, which suggests a link to the tombs.

From myth to pseudohistory: the birth of Druidism

In *Les Origines gauloises* (The Origins of the Gauls) published in 1796, La Tour d'Auvergne wrote of the dolmens, "On such altars, where art and nature made their peace, the Gauls, according to Diodorus of Sicily, swore to their treaties; and here the Druids, their priests, made sacrifices to the gods, most often choosing humans as their victims." This explains the human bones found at the base of pillars of dolmens. La Tour d'Auvergne also notes that Caesar wrote of calling the Druids together at Carnac, among the stone "monuments." Thus the idea of a "historic" Druidism took hold. It was no less fictitious than William Stukeley's poetic-religious Druidism, in the first half of the 18th century.

Chyndonax and Arch-Druid are the name and title

Authors of antiquity created the concept of a Druid as a sage and priest who presided over sacrifices, arbitrated disputes, and, endowed with great poetic power, spoke for the gods in Celtic society. Beginning in the 18th century, the image of the Druid as a priest with long white hair and a full beard, wearing a flowing robe, became associated with the megaliths, giving Druids a religious and ritual dimension. For a long time it was this romantic vision that shaped the study of these monuments. In the images that stemmed from this tradition, Druids were seen as clergy in the religion of the great stones. Below: a fanciful Druidic scene in front of a dolmen.

assumed by William Stukeley (1687–1765), an imaginative Lincolnshire physician and antiquarian who thought he saw the Druidic symbols of a patriarchal society in the landscape of Avebury and Stonehenge in southern England. In 1724 he published *Itinerarium Curiosum* (Itinerary of Curiosities). Far from providing a historical

Discoveries of human skeletal remains in the dolmens have lent credence to the theory that the monuments were altars for human sacrifice—a theme illustrated in this etching by Gustave Doré (above). The 19th century gave us the image of the Druid priestess (left, in a painting by Armand La Roche), holding a sickle to cut mistletoe—a practice noted by Caesar in *The Gallic Wars*. The word *druid* itself may derive from the Greek *drus*, meaning "oak on which mistletoe grows." Pliny wrote that gathering mistletoe was linked to a magic healing ritual and was ideally carried out six days after a new moon.

analysis of ancient texts that dealt with Druids, this book presents Stukeley's attempt to rally disparate faiths around the glory of Christ; he included Judaism and Druidism, which he considered a patriarchal form of Christianity.

The Druid-Sacrifice of Yule-tide.

Stukeley delin. 1759.

William Stukeley (above) had himself depicted as Chyndonax, the Arch-Druid, and tried to combine Christianity and Judaism with the religion of the Druids as he reconstructed it. His religious philosophy was the source of another invented religion, ophiolatry, the cult of the serpent. Stukeley discerned the shape of this animal in the alignments of standing stones, particularly at Avebury, in the south of England (left, center, and opposite).

The theocratic authority of William Stukeley

According to Stukeley's history of the world, the time had come to reconcile the idolatry of the Phoenicians and Druids with the teachings of Moses, Plato, and the Protestant Anglican Church. To him, the enormous scale of the megalithic stone circles symbolized the authority of the Father of a primal religion, from which came the Savior in the guise of a serpent, as represented in the alignments of the monoliths at Avebury. According to Stukeley, the cult of the serpent was central to the megalithic religion. In 1781 Henry Hurle, a follower of Stukeley's, created the Ancient Order of Druids, which still holds its annual meeting at Stonehenge on the summer solstice.

Toward the end of his life, Stukeley met the Scottish poet James Macpherson, the "translator" (in fact the inventor) of the fictitious 3rd-century Gaelic poet Ossian, who set off a craze for romantic fantasy and all things Celtic. There was a widespread interest at this time in the peculiar syncretism of Celtic and Christian mythology. The strong influence exerted by the Druidic priest Stukeley on the poet, William Blake, typifies the intellectual striving of Judeo-Christian Jerusalem and its priests, associated with Avebury and Stonehenge and the Celtic Druids. The poet adopted the excitement that inspired a golden age, and the priest revealed the sacred order.

The Druidism that Stukeley invented is, then, a completely original idea. It has nothing to do with the actual Druids, Gallic priests known to Caesar in the 1st century BC—and was created a full millennium and a half after the last ceremonial use of the megaliths.

The Druid sacrifice of the vernal Equinox.

Stukeley delin. 1759.

In this image steeped in religious iconography, in 1759 Stukeley presented the Druidical sacrifices at Stonehenge both as a kind of Christian crucifixion (the human sacrificed as Christ was on the cross) and as a pagan ritual slaughter (the animal on the pyre).

From the Isiac Table.

Druidism, Celtomania, and sectarianism

The mystical Druidism Stukeley promoted tended to be quite inclusive. At the turn of the 20th century, however, gatherings at the solar temple of Stonehenge inspired the crowds to form separate sects. On 24 August 1905 the Albion Lodge of the Ancient Order of Druids met at the site for the first time for a mass initiation of 650 to 700 lodge brothers, who had to know the secret password, as well as 256 novices. The ceremony began with a huge feast and featured a performance of "The March of the Druids," composed especially for the occasion. Other associations of Druids began to spread throughout the British Isles and France. In this spirit, Druids

In the wake of a Druidic renaissance, enthusiasts would gather at Stonehenge. The revival found a particularly spectacular expression in the ceremony of 24 August 1905.

converged on the stone of Pontypridd Rocking, an event authorities feared might have political consequences. In 1910 the Labour Party organized a demonstration around the same stone.

In Cornwall, starting in 1928, bards wearing blue robes would officiate at ceremonies from the center of the circle of standing stones at Boscawen-Un. Likewise, Stonehenge continued to be a common destination for followers of the Druidic cult. On 21 June 1914, the Grand Druid organized a meeting there but was forced to leave the area, and the meeting was halted. Since then the state, which took over ownership of Stonehenge, has officially protected Druid solstice

Stonehenge became the preferred setting for a rite in which participants cloaked in long white robes would brandish crooks and long sticks. Although quite typical of early-20th-century invented religions, such a staging has nothing to do with ancient or prehistoric rituals, about which we know almost nothing.

observers against any unrest caused by outsiders or members of the group itself. In 1969 two thousand motorcyclists joined the Druids in their celebration of the sun. In 1974 the annual sun rite attracted members of many other religions and special interest groups including Buddhists, Muslims, Christians, Earth worshipers, environmentalists, followers of a South Sea Island deity, and even some who follow the Sioux religion. The crowd was enough of a threat that the ceremony had to be broken off.

In Brittany Druids haunt such hallowed places as the megalithic tomb of Merlin in the Brocéliande woods, where esoteric worship and the celebration of Arthurian legend converge. Other Druidic groups meet in the Celtic forest of Carnutes, unrelated to any megaliths. Similarly, the

In the dolmen chamber of La Table des Marchands (Locmariaquer, Brittany), the headstone slab is decorated with symbolic crooks. Such motifs are faithfully rendered— if not explained— in 19th-century books. In our time, the myth of the menhir lives on, even finding its way into the comic book *Asterix.* The words on the stone read "Souvenir of Armorica [Brittany]."

A new dawn for the Stonehenge Druids' ritual

Druids of the forest of St.-Germain-en-Laye, near Paris, worship the sun and ancient trees. New sects of Druidism continue to be formed. The megaliths are a constant source of esoteric inspiration with sometimes ambiguous connotations.

The subjectivity of this approach to the great stones is such that the marks chipped into some of the slabs and representative of megalithic art—one of the keys to understanding the intentions of the builders—are barely reported or remarked upon by the Druids. Since the marks are incomprehensible, they are of no interest to Celtic enthusiasts. In the 19th century, however, after visiting Gavrinis in the Gulf of Morbihan (Brittany), the author Prosper Mérimée, who was a student of archaeology, expressed his confusion at the ornamented slabs "covered with bizarre designs, curves, lines, straight, broken, sketched, and combined in a hundred different ways."

The Druidic cult endures at Stonehenge (above, a gathering on 22 June 1987, the day after the summer solstice). Observation and research conducted on the site have piqued the interest of new sects and archaeologists alike. The mystery of the solar cycle—and the lunar cycle as well—offers these white-clad Druids a chance to meditate and surround themselves with a group of sun worshipers.

"Speak! Speak to me," the Abbot Mahé, canon of Vannes, France, beseeched the megaliths in 1825. This eager curiosity was shared by his colleagues in a new society called the Antiquarians, devoted to the study of early history, especially the megaliths.

CHAPTER 2
ANTIQUARIANS AND SCHOLARS

Their passion for megaliths drove the Antiquarians to study the monuments in their original sites (right, at Gordon's Edge, Great Britain) and to undertake the first excavations (opposite, at Udleire, Denmark).

Fired by rationalism

At the beginning of the 19th century, Jacques de Cambry challenged William Stukeley's poetic-religious fantasies and championed the revolutionary rationalism of the Antiquarians. To get the stones to "speak," the Antiquarians argued that more attention had to be paid to concrete detail. This meant using a scientific approach: geological research, exploration of portions of monuments that were still buried, and concern for the stones' archaeological and astronomical context. In the year 1805 the Celtic Academy was born, with de Cambry as its first president. In 1814 it was transformed into the Royal Society of French Antiquarians, a change illustrating the shift toward a more historical approach.

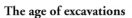

Beginning in 1830, the government of King Louis-Philippe accepted the need to appoint an inspector for the supervision and classification of monuments. In the course of his travels, the first Inspector General of Historic Monuments, Prosper Mérimée, discovered that—in Brittany in particular—the prehistoric stones demonstrated a real sense of architecture. In 1867 the prehistorians gathered at a convention in Paris chose the term *megalith*, proposed by the newly created Polymath Society of Morbihan (Brittany). In 1879 the French Minister of Fine Arts incorporated the Committee for the Special Preservation of Megalithic Monuments into the Commission of Historic Monuments.

Among the treasures amassed from the barrows in the Salisbury region, where Stonehenge is also located, are the dagger ornaments and gold jewelry on these pages. They date to the Bronze Age, around 2000 BC,

The age of excavations

Human remains had been discovered at Stonehenge around 1600, but at that time the Church considered it a sacrilege to exhume them. Not until the early 19th century were Sir Richard Colt Hoare and his excavation director, William Cunnington, able to undertake the exploration of the great tumuli or barrows (mounds) in Salisbury, in southern England. (Explanations of these and other specialized terms may be found in the glossary;

the heyday of the great ceremonial sites. The Salisbury excavations led to the formation of collections, the first classification of artifacts, and the beginning of the process of dating the remains.

Sir Richard Colt Hoare (below, left) and William Cunnington (below) were present at the exploration, by pick and shovel, of a leveled tumulus near Stonehenge (left: watercolor by Philippe Crocher, 1807). Their method, though hasty, had the benefit of supplying physical clues to the meaning

see page 160.) Their research yielded a collection of archaeological artifacts that was presented to the nearby Devizes Museum. These men were followed by General A. L. F. Pitt Rivers in East Dorset, Thomas Bateman in Derbyshire, and Canon William Greenwell in Yorkshire (whose collection is today housed in the British Museum). Thus all of England passed under the close scrutiny of the Antiquarians.

of the monuments and their associated ceremonies.

From that time on, archaeology was recognized as a science and a source of fascination for many, including monarchs. King Frederick VII of Denmark was a particular enthusiast and owned a gravestone exhumed from a trench dug through a Bronze Age barrow. In 1862 near Paris Napoleon III created the National

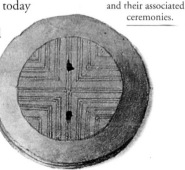

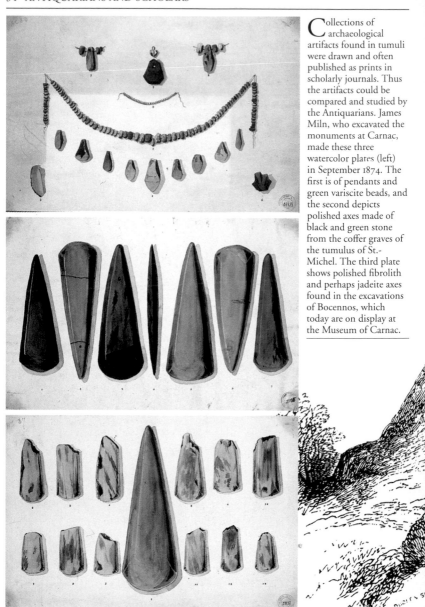

Collections of archaeological artifacts found in tumuli were drawn and often published as prints in scholarly journals. Thus the artifacts could be compared and studied by the Antiquarians. James Miln, who excavated the monuments at Carnac, made these three watercolor plates (left) in September 1874. The first is of pendants and green variscite beads, and the second depicts polished axes made of black and green stone from the coffer graves of the tumulus of St.-Michel. The third plate shows polished fibrolith and perhaps jadeite axes found in the excavations of Bocennos, which today are on display at the Museum of Carnac.

Museum of Antiquities in St.-Germain-en-Laye. It would house, among other collections, one donated by the Baron de Baye from the hypogea (rock-cut tombs) of the Marne region, and another patiently assembled by Paul du Châtellier in the Finistère region of Brittany, where megalithic monuments were excavated. The Museum of the Polymath Society of Morbihan displayed artifacts discovered by its members, while the brand-new museum at Carnac held the collections of James Miln, a Scottish associate of the young Breton archaeologist Zacharie Le Rouzic.

The vogue for excavations initiated a propitious era for the study of megaliths, which was now revived on a more concrete, objective basis. Unfortunately, despite the new empirical approach, the excavators' methods were hurried and destructive. They used three ways of exploring a chamber tomb: digging a shaft from the top to get to the tomb directly; opening up a large section or a trench across the entire mound; or simply razing the whole structure!

Zacharie Le Rouzic (below), by virtue of his rigorous excavation and restoration of the dolmens, ranks as one of the founders of the archaeology of Breton megaliths.

The excavation of a grave mound (in 1844, near Aylesford, England) was practically a surgical operation. In the picture at left, workers with shovel and pick are digging a trench to cut into the mound as far as the central tomb, while the Antiquarians, wearing hats, comment on the work in progress.

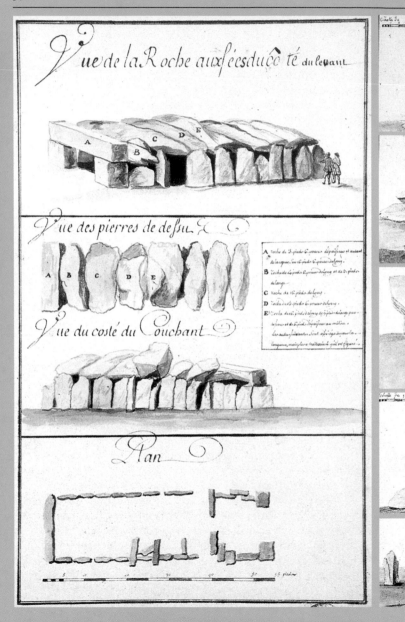

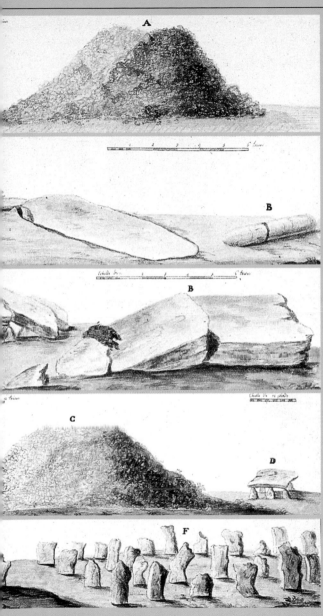

A

B

B

C

D

F

Megalithomania

Christophe-Paul de Robien (1698–1756), a magistrate in the Brittany parliament, can be considered the founder of Breton archaeology. He was the first to study the megalithic monuments, which he identified from the start as tombs. The manuscript of his notes describes the state of the monuments in the 18th century; his three views of the dolmen of La Roche aux Fées (Fairies' Rock) are on the opposite page. Left, center: the monuments of Locmariaquer; in particular the Great Broken Menhir and the dolmen of the Table des Marchands. Left, bottom: the alignments of Carnac.

Following pages: Jacques de Cambry conducted his research at Carnac. Illustrations from his *Le Monde celtique* (The Celtic World, first published in 1805) show him as he examines, measures, and interprets the extravagant shapes of the monoliths. With Cambry, who epitomized the Antiquarians, "megalithomania" was born.

Pl. 4.

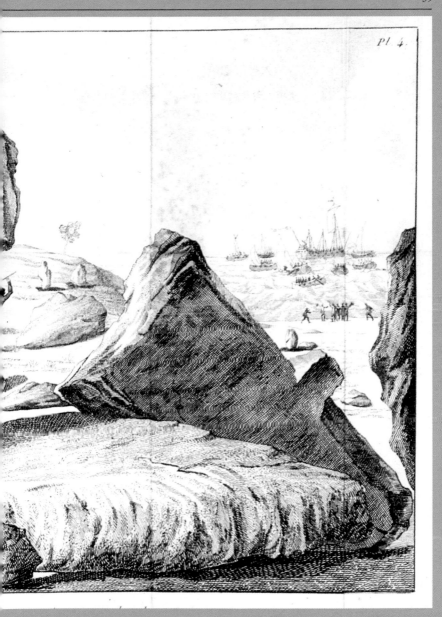

Pl. 3.

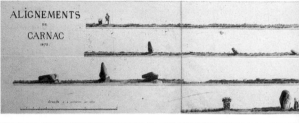

Only the most important remains—known as the "main fossils" because they were representative of the era—were collected, and no precise records were kept. The aim of the excavations was to detect the monument in its original form and date it, while also collecting the best specimens for the museums.

Reports and postcards

As with all structures, the megalithic monuments under study were soon being measured and written up. Starting in 1762, French archaeologist and writer Count Anne-Claude de Caylus insisted that engineers working on bridges and roads draw up plans and profiles of the "Gallic" stones. The

Henri de Cleuziou was known in the 19th century for his books aimed at informing a mass audience about recent work on the origins of the human species. He had a lively interest in the alignments at Carnac, France. At left, his bird's-eye view of the alignment of Le Ménec realistically shows the arrangement of the raised stones in relation to the layout. This map was accompanied by a cross-section of the same alignment (top) with its menhirs still in place in 1873. The lower of the two cross-sections shows Kermario with its menhirs as they appeared in 1874.

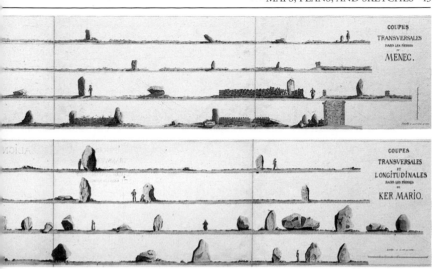

engineer Duchesne made isometric drawings of the famous Pierre Levée (Raised Stone) of Poitiers to obtain more precise dimensions than Rabelais' "twelve toises square and fourteen handspans in thickness." To prevent false reports, the Englishmen W. C. Lukis and Dryden recorded exact measurements of the alignments at Carnac on a map in 1860.

The popularity of gathering numerical data spread. A chart showing the dimensions of fifteen of the most

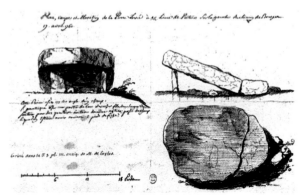

For Count de Caylus, the engineer Duchesne drew the Raised Stone of Poitiers in full frontal view, in profile, and from above (left). De Caylus' archaeology masterwork remains his *Recueil d'antiquités égyptiennes, étrusques, grecques, romaines et gauloises* (Collection of Egyptian, Etruscan, Greek, Roman, and Gallic Antiquities), published in seven volumes in Paris (1752–68). In it he states that "antique monuments are likely to expand our knowledge" as much as the writings of historians can. The methodical drawings in these volumes may be considered to have established a typological and archaeological way of thinking.

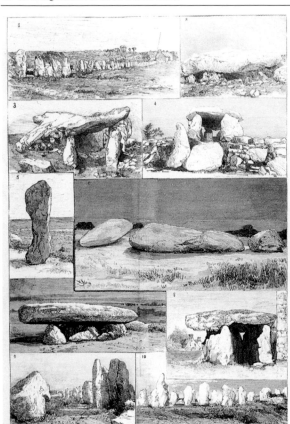

Original and impassioned spirits, the Antiquarians would gather in learned societies, which were springing up throughout Europe. By instituting an Inspection of Historic Monuments in 1830, the French government made official the concern to preserve the patrimony of which the megaliths were part. The same concern for preservation was found in the British Isles, in Denmark, in Germany, and on the Iberian peninsula in the 19th century. The next step was state ownership of the monuments, ensuring more effective protection and display. The montage on the left includes ten pictures from 1888 of some of the megalithic monuments purchased by the French government, including the alignments of Carnac, the famous Great Broken Menhir of Locmariaquer, and several dolmens that had been propped up in preparation for preservation work.

imposing megaliths was published by archaeologist Gabriel de Mortillet. Leading the list was the Great Broken Menhir, estimated to weigh 340 tons and reach a height of 68 feet (21 meters). Angular measurements for the alignments and tomb entrances were of interest to Captain de Vasseau Devoir, a seaman who sought to relate the monuments' architecture to the stars. In 1894 de Mortillet tallied 6,192 megaliths in France, 3,450 of them in Morbihan. In the British Isles, there were 900 circles of standing stones.

Interest in megaliths spread from experts to the public as picture postcards were produced; they were

especially popular around the year 1900. One study has recorded 1,200 cards depicting monuments of Brittany and several colorful individuals. The phototype process, a precursor of offset printing, appeared in 1890 and permitted a faithful reproduction of each important monument and its surrounding landscape to be made.

Trilithon at Elieb. From a Drawing by Dr. Barth.

Universal phenomenon or megalithic religion?

At the close of the 19th century, the discovery of monoliths outside Western Europe, along with analogical research that suggested a kinship among the monuments, raised the possibility of a widespread ancient megalithic

Dolmen at Rajunkoloor. From a drawing by Colonel Meadows Taylor.

RUDE STONE MONUMENTS

religion. According to this school of thought, seagoing missionary priests spread the faith to every continent starting from Egypt, Mesopotamia, or Greece, cradles of such giant structures as the pyramid, ziggurat, and tholos. In 1872 James Fergusson synthesized international research in *Rude Stone Monuments Throughout the World*. In it he stated that "giants" built megalithic tombs in Korea or India, just as they had in Europe; thus they emerged as heroes of a universal mythology. It was hard to resist the temptation to posit a kinship among the widely scattered monuments.

However, little by little, it became clear that many of these structures had something to do with death and displayed a sense of organization, most apparent in their positioning in relation to the stars. Then, starting in the 1950s, the development of physical-chemical techniques for dating drew attention to the significant gaps in time between different megalithic communities.

The success of James Fergusson's *Rude Stone Monuments Throughout the World* was due as much to its text, which demonstrated the universality of megaliths, as to its meticulous illustrations showing largely unknown monuments, sometimes with a human figure to indicate scale. Seen at top is a "trilith" at Tripoli (in fact, an ancient olive oil press!); above, a large megalithic cave in India.

Left: a dolmen in the Caucasus with a porthole slab is reminiscent of some gallery graves in the Paris basin.

Stonehenge. This is said to have been built as a Temple for the worship of the Sun 3,700 years ago. Others say that it was erected in the reign of Aurelius Ambrosius King of Britain, 490, to commemorate the defeat of the Britons by Hengist. The stones are supposed to have been brought from Ireland by the Magic of Merlin.

STONEHENGE.

Dear E. I daresay you have heard of this place. It is 20 mls from here
With love. A. M.

Souvenirs of megaliths

178. CARNAC. — Dolmen et Menhirs de Kermario.

Marcel 18 Juillet 1902

CARNAC. — Alignements du Ménec.

CARNAC — Dolmen de Mané-Kerioned

24/7 04
Marcel

More than 1,200 postcards depicting megalithic monuments from Brittany alone were produced between 1900 and 1926. The monuments had become the pride of some communities (on this page, Carnac). The trend spread to other parts of Europe. The great attraction of the postcards is that they show the monuments in their landscape, with children, women, and men in traditional costumes providing a relative scale. This stock of early images, their quality depending on the camera work and the printing, provided documentation that has been essential to a modern understanding of these vast sites. The photographs taken by Adrien de Mortillet (son of Gabriel) in 1893 near Sartène, in southern Corsica, and featuring the dolmen of Fontanaccia (pages 46-47) demonstrate the interest in megaliths throughout that region. Opposite: as these postcards attest, Stonehenge, in England, has long been a tourist site.

B etween the 5th and 2nd millennia BC, the building of megaliths in Western Europe underwent several phases of development, each marked by a specific style of architecture. This applied to dolmens as well as menhirs. Held in awe throughout the centuries, these burial chambers and standing stones were sometimes transformed and reconstructed.

CHAPTER 3

THREE THOUSAND YEARS OF ARCHITECTURE

The portico dolmen with two columns supporting an enormous covering block—a style of architecture dating from the 4th millennium BC—is characteristic of northwestern Ireland (opposite, the dolmen of Groleck). Originally the blocks were covered with the loose stones of a tumulus, which modern excavations have uncovered (right, at Les Fouillages in Guernsey).

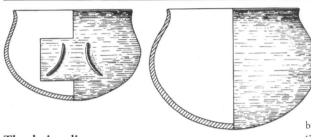

The dating dispute

In 1955 on the Plouézoc'h promontory, north of Morlaix in Finistère, Brittany, the long tumulus of Barnenez—230 feet (70 meters) in length, with eleven passage graves, constructed in a circular pattern of drystone topped with slabs—was threatened with destruction. A similar mound nearby had already been destroyed. The threat to Barnenez made it critical to scientifically date these enormous stone relics. The carbon 14 dating technique, devised in 1949 by the American chemist Willard Frank Libby, was used, and the results obtained on samples of charcoal amazed the scientific community: it turned out that the monument had been built in two stages in the middle of the 5th millennium BC.

Carbon 14 dating on wood charcoal found on the ancient ground of a monument on the Isle of Carn in the Gulf of Finistère (below) indicates that this site was in use between 4400 and 4200 BC; the dates were confirmed by the study of the ceramics found there (left). This pile of building stones covering funerary chambers is known as a cairn—hence the name of the island.

Several archaeologists refused to accept the finding, arguing that the charcoal, which came from old ground, might predate the monument's construction. However, similar dates were found for samples taken from two other tumuli

The Les Fouillages monument on Guernsey (above) was contemporaneous with the first farmers, around 4500–4000 BC, a period identified by ceramics with perforated decorations. Originally, a mound surrounded by large blocks covered central aligned coffers.

in Finistère, on the islands of Guennoc and Carn.

Several years later, in 1973, at Bougon (Deux-Sèvres, France) in chalky land favorable to the preservation of human bones, carbon dating was performed on bones from two tombs (Tumuli E and Fo). The resulting dates ranged from 5040 to 4390 BC. Evidently, while the construction of megaliths began in Brittany and in west-central France around 4500 BC, in some places it began even earlier.

The age of the megaliths—as old as they are—was later confirmed, particularly by thermoluminescence dating, which determines age by measuring the amount of phosphorescence old material generates after being gently heated. This method was tested on a variety of samples, including those of monument I of Poço de Gateira and a neighboring tomb in Portugal. Huge megaliths, such as the dolmen of Alberite (Cadiz, Spain), were confirmed by carbon 14 dating to have been on the Iberian peninsula since the 5th millennium, which poses the problem of their independent development in certain locales. Such scientifically-arrived-at dating seriously calls into question the possibility of any influence from the East, particularly that of Mycenean Greece

Megalithism is one of the most ancient forms of sacred architecture. Evidence of this is provided by this diagram comparing (top to bottom) the first monumental constructions in the Middle East (tower of Jericho, Mesopotamian ziggurat, Egyptian mastaba and pyramids) and the great tumuli, tumuli with square megalithic chambers, gallery graves, and circles of raised stones.

(the tomb of the Atreides). French writer André Malraux summed up the sudden importance commanded by megalithic constructions when, on a visit to the monument of Barnenez, he awarded it the title "Megalithic Parthenon." After that, the question of where megalithic architecture came from took on new urgency.

From the "proto-megaliths"...

The communal character of the burial coffers of the Mesolithic period (8th to 5th millennia BC) in Téviec and in Hoédic (Morbihan, Brittany) recalls the cemeteries at Muge in Portugal and the public graves of Bögebakken and Skateholm in Denmark. Was the 5th millennium, then, the beginning of megalithic burial? The use of a large slab covering graves dates to the second half of the 5th millennium—there are graves with one or two skeletons (around Malesherbes, Loiret, France) or with many skeletons placed face down (Pontcharaud, near Clermont-Ferrand, Puy-de-Dôme). But these slabs did not reach the monumental proportions of megalithic tombs.

Megalithic forms from the 5th millennium BC are found on the Atlantic coast of the Iberian peninsula, from Galicia to Portugal. Raised stones ornamented with chipped-out circles, arranged as a cromlech, in Almendres, near Evora, Portugal (opposite), are similar to monuments in Brittany and Great Britain. The large dolmens of Viseu, also in Portugal (below), are both unique in the layout of their chambers and similar to other large megalithic structures of the European Atlantic coast.

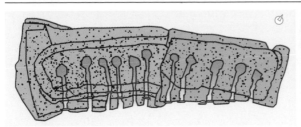

Coffers like that of St.-Martin-la-Rivière (Vienne, France) were also built into a below-ground pit; in western Europe they might have been protected by mounds, as in the tumulus complex of Les Fouillages (Guernsey), the long tumuli in the manner of St.-Michel and Moustoir at Carnac (Morbihan), Mané-er-Hroeck and Mané-Lud (Locmariaquer), and Tumiac (Arzon). Thus the grand "proto-megalithic" structures combined the funerary coffer—of Mesolithic origins in the Atlantic zone and of ancient Neolithic origins in Switzerland—with the long monumental tumulus. The long tumulus is a very old form dating from the first half of the 5th millennium in Brittany and in west-central France, perhaps related to the long, fortified necropolis structures of Haute-Bonny, in Rots (Calvados), and of Passy (Yonne) in the eastern part of the Paris basin.

The tumulus of Barnenez, France (above), has all the characteristics of megalithic architecture: monumental proportions, the presence of communal burial places (diagram above, left), and the use of large stones (left, the interior of a chamber). The western part of the tumulus was constructed around 4700 BC and the eastern, 400 years later.

...to the Megaliths

The tradition of the long proto-megalithic tumulus lasted throughout the entire 4th millennium BC in Denmark and Great Britain. But by the middle of the

5th millennium BC, the tumulus of Barnenez, while a part of this tradition, had broken new ground. In the place of coffers, it had burial chambers made of large stones accessible to the outside by a passage; the chambers were fit for communal rites.

Three criteria—a tumulus, communal burial rites, and large stones—distinguish megalithic architecture. The beginnings of megalithic construction seem closely tied to the settling of a new class of farmers around 6000 BC. They brought their way of life—and their pursuit of fertile soil—with them from the Near East. When their migrations were halted by the Atlantic coast, these farmers had to adapt to a permanently settled way of life. Using megalithic

The tumulus of St.-Michel at Carnac, now crowned with a chapel, once had burial coffers with no entry passages, an archaic form compared to tombs in Barnenez.

monuments to organize ancestor worship, these people legitimized their territorial ownership while affirming their cultural identity.

Typology of megalithic architecture

For the last fifty years, systematic inventories have been compiled following large excavation campaigns in northern Germany, Ireland, the British Isles, Brittany, the Iberian peninsula, and Malta. From the comparison of observations made during these explorations, archaeologists were able to establish a classification of megalithic architectural styles in Western Europe—of the dolmens (what remained of the tombs after the protective tumulus had disappeared) and the menhirs.

The chamber dolmen is a simple closed coffer or cist set out in a square or rectangle of modest dimensions that was formed by slabs covering the remains of one or, most often, several skeletons. This simple form of tumulus, buried or covered, is very widespread in Monchique (Algarve, Portugal), Carnac, Chamblandes (Switzerland), Denmark, and England.

In its next phase, the chamber dolmen, properly defined, is characterized by rather large dimensions —7 to 20 feet (2 to 6 meters) in length and some-

The simplest burial design is that of the coffer or cist bounded by slabs and protected by a tumulus edged with large stones (uppermost diagram). The photograph below shows the tumulus remains of Manio III at Carnac,

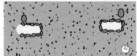

with its border of stones and central coffer. The next group are burial chambers, either circular or four-sided, with an entry passage. The two diagrams directly above and the photograph at left show the necropolis of Champ-Chalon (Charente-Maritime).

times more. It is accessible by a passage or vestibule from the entrance built onto the facade of the tumulus. The tomb was accordingly closed or opened to allow for new burials, reflecting its function as a communal burial site. Archaeologists have based their classification on the floor plan of the chamber.

The dolmen with a round chamber and a passageway is constructed of drystone with a corbeled ceiling. Slabs reinforce the passageway and the sides of the chamber. This architectural model, often found in western France (for example, at Barnenez), first appeared at the beginning of the 5th millennium BC, but continued into the 4th. As large slabs were used more and more commonly to replace drystone, the circular arrangement of the passage became hexagonal in shape, as in Portugal.

The dolmen with a rectangular chamber and a passageway signaled the evolution toward a more distinct use of megaliths, as both the chamber and the cover were constituted of large slabs. The increasing size of the slabs in effect defines the stage of megalithic construction.

The increasing number of chambers around the same passageway evolved into the Irish court dolmens: two to four simple rectangular chambers aligned in the same tumulus with a concave facade forming a "courtyard," and also transept designs like that of

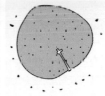

From a simple, four-sided design, the passage grave evolved through more complex phases, such as the transept model (above: Newgrange, around 3000 BC, along with a sketch of the tumulus complex and a layout of the tomb). There is a disproportion between functional interior architecture and the exterior monumentality, which was designed to make an impression on the community.

Newgrange (and also often found in the Orkney Islands, England, and the Loire region of France).

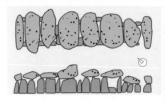

The widening and elongation of the dolmen chamber are evident in the designs typical of the Angoulême region of France as well as the region of Angers, the site of the most megalithic of all dolmens: those of La Roche aux Fées (Fairics' Rock) and Bagneux, 57 by 14 feet at ground level and 8 feet high (17.4 by 4.3 meters, and 2.4 meters high). Similar giant proportions also are found in dolmens of southern Spain, at La Cueva de Menga (Antequera) and El Pozuelo (La Huelva).

The elongation of the chambers gives rise to architectural forms with passageways. The elongated dolmen, such as that of Midhowe in the Orkney Islands, has an axial passage, while in northern Germany and the Netherlands the majority of dolmens have lateral passages. In Brittany a unique elongated and angled dolmen (Pierres Plates in Locmariaquer) also has a lateral passage. Whether it is buried or

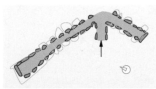

L a Roche aux Fées (Fairies' Rock, photograph and diagram above) with its rectangular chamber (65 by 20 feet, or 19.8 by 6.1 meters, and 13 feet [4 meters] high outside) represents the high point of megalithic construction in Western Europe at the beginning of the 4th millennium. Its axial passageway is shorter and lower than the chamber, which is set off by a portico. The elongation of the chamber recurs at the end of the 4th millennium in Brittany, with the long and angled dolmen of the Pierres Plates in Locmariaquer (photograph and diagram at left).

The gallery grave of around 3000 BC was an elongated passage grave, which was bordered and most often covered with slabs of the same height. Entrance, on the axis of the monument, was through a vestibule which is in some places separated from the chamber by a porthole slab. Some gallery graves, as in the Paris basin, were underground (below, La Pierre Turquaise at St.-Martin-du-Tertre, Val-d'Oise, with sandstone slab outcroppings). Others (for example in Brittany, Belgium, and Westphalia) were constructed at ground level and covered by a mound.

The Main Megalithic Regions of Europe

4000 BC
3000 BC
2000 BC

Callanish
Stenness-Brogar
Maes Howe

Slewcairn

Tustrup
Lougherew   Knowth
Newgrange
Bygholm Norremark
Groenhoej
Kivik
Trollasten
Gnewitz
Liepen
Frauenmark

West Kennet   Avebury
Maiden Castle   Stonehenge
Fussel's Lodge
Bush Barrow
La Chaussée-Tirancourt

Sarnov

Guennoc   Barnenez
Carn
Colpo   Tressé
St.-Just   Epône
Les Mounouards, Le Mesnil-sur-Oger
Le Razet, Coizard

Liscuis, Laniscat
Essé
Locmariaquer
Carnac   Gavrinis
Arzon
Dissignac
Benon   Bougon
La Boixe   Chenon
Bagneux   Passy
Aillevans
Chamblandes
Sion
Pontcharaud 2
Lugasson

Roaix
Lamalou, Rouet
Pépieux   Arles-Fontvielle
Orgon

Carapito 1

Palmela
Poço de Gateira
Filitosa   Cucuruzzu
Fontanaccia
El Tudons   Anghelu Ruju   Li-Muri
La Atalaia
Palmeira 4, Monchique
Serra d'Alto
Gaudo
Antequera   Los Millares
Almizaraque
San Andrea Priu
El Barranquete
Castellucio

Roknia
Hal Saflieni, Malta
Gastel
Ggantija, Gozo
Tarxien, Hagar Kim, Malta

not, the gallery grave has an antechamber between a short passage and the chamber as its defining feature.

This design of the gallery graves, with a four-sided chamber, antechamber, and very short entry passage, is found in hypogea in the Paris basin and near the Mediterranean (around Arles and Sardinia). Their peak was around 3000 BC.

Other hypogea with circular chambers are found in Portugal, Malta, Crete, and Palestine. Near Lisbon several necropolises in the form of hypogea—those in Palmela are the best known— have a perfectly circular chamber and a vestibule with concave

walls. In Malta, the hypogeum of Hal Saflieni is terraced on three subterranean levels, which were dug out during several stages of use. All together, about twenty chambers contain seven thousand skeletons. The hypogeum in Crete is a prototype of the tholos tomb, that of Kephala, for example, which heralds the tomb of the Atreides in Mycenae—a monument dating from

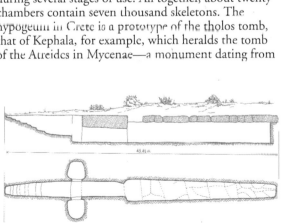

The hypogeum of Coizard (Marne) also served as a tomb, with a passageway in the foreground and an antechamber and chamber seen farther back (above). Left: the layout of the hypogeum of Arles, dug into the ground and covered with large slabs, reveals the close connection between megaliths and this particular kind of monument, which has Mediterranean origins.

43.46 m

around 1300 BC, which used to be thought of as the beginning of western megalithic construction.

Various kinds of menhirs

When it comes to raised stones, classification is much more straightforward: menhirs are either isolated, aligned along a straight axis, or placed in a circle. The alignments of Carnac are composed of several groupings—Le Ménec, Kermario, and Kerlescan.

Like the megalithic tombs, menhirs were part of the grand settings of ceremonies dedicated to ancestors. The stones were set apart or aligned along a specific celestial axis. Avebury, not far from Stonehenge, is an arrangement of three large circles of raised stones; the largest, which surrounds the other two, is set up along a wide ditch.

These are associated with menhirs laid out in ovals or rectangles whose major axes run along a southeast and southwest path, in other words, in the direction of sunrise to sunset.

Certain individual menhirs may have had a specific significance, such as the orientation stone called the Heel Stone at Stonehenge. In addition, raised stones can sometimes be said to function as tombs, as some were sanctified by virtue of the human

At St.-Just (Ille-et-Vilaine), collapsed menhirs have been used as walls of funerary coffers (inset, left).

Statue-menhirs and the torres of Corsica and the Balearic Islands

In Corsica the first megalithic monuments—for example, the coffers of Porto-Vecchio and the dolmen of Fontanaccia (near Sartène)—date from the 4th and 3rd millennia BC. Torres, towers associated with statue-menhirs from the Bronze Age (2nd millennium BC), make a spectacular grouping at Filitosa (opposite). On Minorca, in the Balearic Islands, there are two kinds of megalithic monuments, architectural designs for funerals and ceremonies: the taula (above, left), which is the remains of a corbeled building, and the naveta, a four-sided tower like the one from Els Tudons (below, left).

Sardinia's giant tombs

Rich in megalithic monuments, Sardinia developed hypogea decorated with anthropomorphic and bovine motifs beginning in the 5th millennium. Giants' tombs are a Sardinian specialty. An elongated tomb made of slabs (opposite, below) is entered through a doorway cut in the base of a monumental carved slab (left) integrated into a concave facade (opposite, above). Sardinia also has standing stones, in particular very stylized conical menhir statues depicting female breasts. The nuraghe is a massive tower protecting an interior chamber that may have served a religious purpose.

Temples and hypogea of Malta

Insularity explains the originality of the megalithic architecture of the two neighboring islands of Malta and Gozo, south of Sicily. Burial hypogea like that of Hal Saflieni (opposite, below), cut into the rock, imitate the architectural details of the temples outside the cloverleaf site, which today comprises roofless ruins (at left, above and below, the temple of Mnadira). The islands shared a religion dominated by the mother goddess; the Sleeping Woman of Hal Saflieni (below) is found in all these monuments of the 4th millennium, and especially in the Xaghra Stone Circle, a recently discovered ceremonial structure.

bones buried at their base; others were used—during a subsequent phase of their veneration—in the construction of a small funerary coffer. This is the case of the alignment of Cojoux (St.-Just, France).

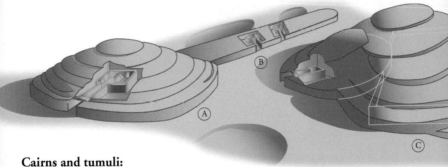

Cairns and tumuli: composite monuments used as necropolis and as ceremonial center

The spectacular, monumental long tumuli are associated with architectural forms that are basically megalithic. The monuments at Douhet (Charente-Maritime) and Gros Dognon (Charente) like those in Morbihan (Brittany), and in England and Denmark, are gigantic. Though they do not present truly megalithic funerary structures, they are sometimes composite. This is true of the long barrow of Bygholm Norremark (Denmark), which reveals five phases of building in the course of the 4th millennium, only the last of which is truly megalithic.

Conversely, in the necropolis of Bougon (Deux-Sèvres), which occupies about five acres in the center of a Neolithic site some six miles in diameter, megalithic tombs are found in a round tumulus augmented in a second building phase by a rectangular stone mass that gives them the appearance of giant barrows. This method —spectacularly juxtaposing five composite mounds—amplified their monumental impact within the necropolis.

At the cairn of Petit Mont (Arzon, on the coast of the Gulf of Morbihan, Brittany), four phases of

The phenomenon of megaliths is cumulative in nature. The function of the monuments was handed on from one generation to the next, to preserve the teachings of the earliest ancestors. The four phases of construction of the tumulus of the Petit Mont (Arzon, below), cover the three thousand years of the Neolithic age.

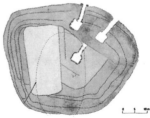

- - - - - - -   1st phase
              2nd phase
              3rd phase
              4th phase

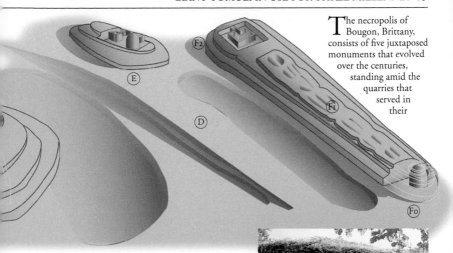

The necropolis of Bougon, Brittany, consists of five juxtaposed monuments that evolved over the centuries, standing amid the quarries that served in their

construction can be seen. The initial monument is a mound with a central ditch—for burial, no doubt—measuring 175 feet (53 meters) in length and dated 4580 to 4440 BC, upon which a rectangular cairn was built. This cairn, in turn, is flanked by a monumental addition known as cairn II, intended as protection for a first megalithic passage chamber, marked off by a fallen anthropomorphic stele. Cairn III, which covers the preceding ensemble, forms a trapezoidal stone structure 175 feet long. Its front opens onto the passageways of two new megalithic tombs. Various fragments of bell-shaped vases show that the ceremonial use of the monument lasted until the end of the 3rd millennium.

The Locmariaquer complex in Brittany reaches a length of about 1,650 feet (503 meters)—more than 5,000 feet (1,524 meters) if we include the extended, angled chamber of Pierres Plates, the most recent and southernmost section. This site was renovated at the north and south, first with the addition of the great coffer tumulus of Mané-Lud (and perhaps also Mané-er-Hroeck), then with the series of giant standing stones whose fragments are found at the Table des Marchands, Er Grah, and Mané Rutual.

construction. The earliest chambers, E and Fo, date from 4700 BC, while those known as B and C are from 4300 BC. The great dolmens covered with a slab weighing 32 tons (F2, north of tumulus F) and 90 tons (A) were erected around 4000 BC and reused as burial chambers around 3000 BC, a proof of the long-term use and veneration of this sanctuary.

Other vast landscapes have also been turned into immense sanctuaries, such as the famous site of Carnac which, with its standing-stone alignments and circles, tumuli, and megalithic tombs, occupies a stretch of country two miles long. The excavations at Cojoux (St.-Just) have also uncovered megalithic architectural sites extending over several miles.

Recycling and recovery: reusing the giant idols

When, in 1983, Charles Tanguy LeRoux removed the covering slab of the chamber of Gavrinis (Brittany), he looked down on the carving of a 10-foot-long ox with curving horns, the upper portion of another ox, and the lower part of an ax-plow interrupted by two clear breaks in this intermediate block. Examination of the orthogneiss rock, originating from an outcropping 10 to 15 miles (17 to 25 km) distant, led to identification of the two other pieces of the original whole 3 miles (5 km) from Gavrinis at Locmariaquer. There they were being used to cover the dolmens of Er Grah and the Table des Marchands near the Great Broken Menhir. The first monolith in the reconstruction here measured about 45 feet (13.7 meters) in length and weighed 200 tons, while the second was 68 feet (21 meters) long and weighed about 340 tons. The excavations at Locmariaquer revealed at least nineteen ditches filled with wedging stones to keep the giant venerated megaliths standing—at least until their systematic destruction and the reuse of their fragments in the building of the dolmens of Morbihan around 4000 BC. Thus the great recovered stones, disproportionate in relation to the architecture of the funeral chambers and passage and decorated with motifs interrupted by breaks, were seen to be blocks removed from giant steles or

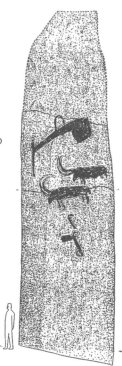

At Locmariaquer nineteen ditches with their wedging stones served as a base for giant menhirs such as the Great Broken Menhir, which was left in place and had been standing (left). The human form sketched below, standing beside another menhir of the same series, gives an idea of their immense scale. Two other decorated monoliths must have been part of this alignment before they were reused in the dolmen of Mané Rutual at Locmariaquer (opposite, below).

Archaeologist C. T. LeRoux unearthed the carving of a 10-foot-long (3 meter) ox (left) on the hidden upper surface of the broken capstone slab of the Gavrinis dolmen. This revelation helped establish a direct link between this slab and the fragment covering the chamber of the Table des Marchands dolmen at Locmariaquer

menhirs. The dolmen of Mané Rutual at Locmariaquer is covered by a broken stele some 13 feet (4 meters) long, decorated with a chipped-out shield idol. In the monument of Petit Mont, at Arzon, a large, 18-foot-tall (5.5 meter) stele with an anthropomorphic profile was apparently raised in front of cairn I. When the monument was extended, cairn II leaned against the earlier one and covered up a new passage chamber designed to lead from the fallen stele, with the lower portion forming the headstone slab and the upper part of the floor of the new structure.

What ideological shift could account for these radical changes? Possibly

(above). On this block, in fact, we can make out the continuation of the picture of the second bull (its feet); its back and horns were found on the block at Gavrinis. The monolith was originally 45 feet high (13.7 meters) and weighed about 200 tons (reconstruction on opposite page). The uppermost block is surely the one that covers the dolmen of Er Grah. The alignment of the giant idols at Locmariaquer must have also included the headstone slab idol of the Table des Marchands, which remained in place.

The decorated slabs of Gavrinis, Brittany (opposite), justly considered the summit of megalithic Breton art, formed the walls of a long passage and of a square chamber. The visible surface is covered in an ornate, "baroque" style with chipped-out lines that repeat certain classic motifs of megalithic Breton art— the female idol associated with the serpent, with the ax, crook, and bow as attributes of male power. At the same time, another artistic style, less strictly regular, dominated by the theme of the radiating sun, is clearly seen at the Petit Mont (Arzon), near Gavrinis. It has affinities with the Irish art from the Boyne River Valley that developed at the end of the 4th millennium. The tomb at Knowth (left), for instance, reveals spirals, radiating and concentric circles, zigzags, diamond shapes, and cup marks, along with one other curious element, feet.

The celestial themes of megalithic art appear both in Ireland (left, a "sundial" on one of the slabs at Knowth) and in Portugal. The sun and moon are painted on the dolmen of Antelas (below left) at Oliveira de Frades (Viseu) and the sun appears on the menhir of Bulhoa (below) at Monsaraz (Alentejo).

tribal rivalries, such as those thought to have occurred at Easter Island? This phenomenon is different in Morbihan because each fragment is reintegrated into a new type of megalithic architecture associated more closely with the funerary ritual. Ancestor worship may have replaced the cult of giant idols. One can only marvel at the energy this must have required, for it was a true revolution in a civilization's beliefs.

Signs and decorations

Perhaps, as excavations suggest, the stone facade of Gavrinis was supplemented by wooden structures. But nothing on the exterior prepares the viewer for the baroque splendor of the decorations covering the slabs in the long access passage to the chamber. The chamber itself is totally covered with

recurring chipped-out designs of axes, crooks, shield idols, arcs, and zigzag patterns that are either interlacing or presented just once (as in the case of the bow and the serpent). It has been proposed that the iconography refers to the emblems of male power (bow, ax, crook) and a female deity (shield idol), possibly in relation to the serpent. The site of Gavrinis, built around 4000 BC, represents the peak of Morbihan art and indeed of all the megalithic art of western France.

The art of the Irish megalithic sites, though equally rich and intricate, is not directly comparable to Gavrinis. The Boyne Valley, north of Dublin, looks like a series of circular mounds, the most famous of which is Newgrange (County Meath). One of the slabs in its chamber is decorated with a large triskelion (a triple-spiral design) illuminated by a sunbeam traversing the passage on the day of the winter solstice. The passage entrance is blocked by a slab decorated with spirals (including an early form of the triskelion), lozenges, and zigzags. Ninety-seven blocks decorated with the same geometric motifs surround the tumulus, which is enclosed in turn by thirty-eight menhirs.

In a neighboring site, at Knowth, the central mound is also enclosed by slabs finely chipped with circular, spiral, oval, or square motifs, or with geometrically fantastical chevrons or zigzags. One of the slabs can serve as a solar clock. The ordered style of Newgrange or Knowth differs from the free style of Loughcrew in northwestern County Meath, though this site shows the same inspiration, based on suns, spiral movements, and sawtoothed interlacings. These monuments appear to date from around 3000 BC, by which time Gavrinis had long since been abandoned.

The Newgrange mound is surrounded by blocks decorated with the so-called celestial motifs that are so common in Irish art (above). The spiral may represent the course of the sun. This block served another function in connection with the sun cycle: placed before the entrance to the passage of the mound on the day of the winter solstice, it allowed the rising sun to shine through an opening just above the passage entrance and reach the innermost wall of the burial chamber.

In the rural village society that arose in Western Europe in the course of the 5th millennium BC, a robust religion—ancestor worship—developed. Megaliths, an important innovation of this society, symbolically protected or evoked the most renowned dead. Technology and ritual demonstrate the vitality of these structures, as well as their remarkable survival.

CHAPTER 4

THE PALACE OF THE DEAD AND OF THE GODS

Megalithic tombs (such as the one at Barnenez, opposite) are sacred monuments; they became sanctuaries by honoring members of leading families who had attained the status of revered ancestors (such as at Lauzet-Ubaye, France, in the dolmen of Villard, right).

In the mass grave of Pontcharaud, France (left), bodies of men, women, and children (about ten in all) lie face down, their heads turned to the side. To keep the dead from moving or returning to daily life, their hands and feet were severed and the bodies were weighed down under heavy slabs. Such funerary practices suggest a fear of the spirits of ancestors.

For one hundred thousand years, humans had concerned themselves with their dead. For the most part, bodies were carefully placed in graves cut out of rock, isolated from the community or near plains dwellings. Huge stones sometimes served to seal off these recesses. The megalithic structures gave birth to an open-air architecture using durable materials (some researchers see this as an attempt to imitate grottoes), intended to hold the remains of ancestors, following complex, constantly renewed rituals. The spirits of the dead, and probably of the gods—necessary to any society that makes use of symbols, as researcher Jacques Cauvin has said—thus inhabited the stones of which the vaults were built or the commemorative standing stone.

Fearsome, protective ancestors: the cult of relics

Megalithic graves were collective, and funerary rites called for a considerable expenditure of energy and a commitment by the whole community. Examination of the tomb of Pontcharaud (before 4000 BC), near Clermont-Ferrand, France, demonstrates the amount of attention that was devoted to the dead as well as the fear

A solemn procession that approached the entrance to a megalithic tomb brandishing torches to penetrate the world of darkness is a romantic evocation of ancient funerary rites (above). Reality was more complex, incorporating secondary rites— symbolic manipulations revealing the intentions of the living toward the departed.

the dead inspired. Feet and hands severed, the bodies were arranged in a prone position in which they could be imagined to move only in one direction—toward the darkness of death. Moreover, heavy rocks were placed on top of them so that they could not escape toward the light. Amputation of the hands and feet must have occurred during secondary rites following death.

These rites evoke the system of symbolism that transformed the corpse into a relic and made the departed an ancestor to be propitiated. It is not rare to find in megalithic tombs the skeletal remains of several bodies, removed from a separate site of presentation, or with reliquary bones severed. In the chamber of tumulus B1 in Bougon, France, for instance, cranial sections were found along with long, aligned bones, representing relics pared down to the essential. They are quite unlike the simple skeletal reductions found at La Chaussée-Tirancourt, France.

The excavation of tomb number 5 at Tagarp, Sweden (above), revealed the structure of the tumulus and its various parts—passage and burial chamber. The megalithic tomb played a dual role. Inside, it was a memorial for the departed. Outside it was a place of worship where, once the tomb chamber had been sealed off, the faithful continued, generation after generation, to honor the memory of ancestors still present through their bones, which had now become relics.

Collective vaults and social distinctions

In the course of the 4th millennium BC, megalithic tombs spread across a good part of Western Europe. Tombs built on a simple square or circular plan were frequent in southern France, Spain, the Pyrenees, the Causses Mountains of central France, Ireland, northern Germany, and Denmark. Other tombs with long chambers—the angled dolmens and the gallery graves of Brittany, the Ile-de-France (north-central France), Belgium, Holland, and Germany—appeared to be more collective vaults. Hypogea, known in the Mediterranean regions as well as in the Marne (northeastern France), show the same ritual traces as those observed in the gallery graves. In the hypogeum at Roaix (Vaucluse, France, 3rd millennium BC), a level containing thirty-five skeletons grouped together—as indicated from a study of the positions of the various skeletal remains—corresponds to the function of an ossuary, perhaps following some wartime carnage. The existence of mass graves is confirmed beginning in the 5th millennium BC, at Talheim, near Stuttgart. It may be that a climate of insecurity encouraged the solidarity exhibited in the collective vaults. The question of human sacrifice is apparently presented in a context of warfare, as at Auzay-les-Chatelliers (Vendée, France).

In most other megalithic monuments, the function of vault or reliquary is associated with secondary rites, practiced for long periods, that reflected social hierarchy.

In Denmark the wooden, thatched-roof houses of the dead identified at Tustrup and Vrone Hede were intended to receive

The two skeletons from Auzay-les-Chatelliers (Vendée, above and opposite, above) show traces of violent death.

The plan of the dolmen of Axevalla, Sweden, with internal compartments grouping the departed by family (above).

the remains of the dead before they were placed in a careful arrangement in the megalithic tomb. Small compartments set off by little slabs, found in the long chambers of Ingelstorp (southern Sweden) and Gnewitz (northern Germany), were designed to house the "packages" of dried bones of ancestors belonging to families of a certain social rank. At Ingelstorp and Hagestad, megalithic tombs of prominent persons—the most impressive ones—were built near the best lands, whereas other, more modest graves were scattered over the less-fruitful terrain reserved for raising pigs and sheep.

In the gallery grave of La Chaussée-Tirancourt, France (below), skeletal remains of one person were gathered against a wall slab, apparently to mark the position of this person among the others.

Megaliths and social hierarchy

The megalithic monument was designed to be seen from afar and play a social and religious role in the midst of a rural

landscape in which farm people were gradually becoming settled. The hierarchy among monuments reflects a real desire to organize the countryside. The monuments at such French sites as Kercado, Dissignac, and Bougon, for example, were integrated since the 5th millennium BC within a certain territory, which was bordered by satellite monuments. Others—for instance, the central tumulus at Hagestad (Sweden), those at Knowth and Newgrange (Ireland), or the one at La Cueva de Romeral (Spain)— served the same function starting in the next millennium. In Jersey the enormous mound of Hougue Bie dominates the other megalithic structures on the island.

The vast central tumulus of Knowth, Ireland (above), contained only two small funerary chambers with a long passage. This monumental scale indicates the importance of the persons buried there; it is emphasized by sixteen small circular satellite mounds, each containing one megalithic grave.

Among the more ancient monuments, inside its mass of stones the cairn of Barnenez shelters the chamber dolmen H, the only one covered with a megalithic slab and the only one with a double chamber and incised decoration. This is proof of a hierarchy among the tombs.

Anthropological studies of skeletons from the more recent continental megalithic tombs (such as the one at La Chaussée-Tirancourt or the long English barrows like that at Hambledon Hill) seem to show that the apparently large number of buried bodies—250 to 300 at the former location and 350 at the latter—represent only a selected portion of the population, if considered over a period of several centuries. There is thus a dual

hierarchy: among persons placed within megalithic tombs, and also among the tombs themselves. The best example of this social, political, and religious organization, according to English archaeologist Colin Renfrew, was surely the monument of Stonehenge, the ceremonial center for several territories, each with its own monumental graves, ceremonial sites, and fortified settlements.

The interior of the megalithic chamber of Hougue Bie on the island of Jersey (left) shows the power of this architecture of raw blocks. From their geology, we know that the blocks come from various areas of the island, suggesting that secondary populations might have participated in the building on behalf of a dominant central group. Mobilization of the collective energies necessary for the building of megaliths would have required some social and possibly religious hierarchy. Even if a certain equality tended to prevail among the members of a given population residing in similar, rather modest houses, we may speculate that the building of the tombs and sanctuaries depended on an elite class that controlled political power, diplomacy, learning, and the secrets of the gods. In this sense, only a few persons organized the collective works and presided over the ancestor worship. At Stonehenge, a major sacred monument, the priest presumably enjoyed considerable power.

Trepanning: surgery or ritual treatment of human bones

The practice of trepanning (perforation) human skulls reveals a lively concern with knowing about human

The megaliths of Senegal

The necropolis of Sine-Ngayene in southern Senegal is marked by circles and standing stones (left). Within each of the circles, a filled-in ditch contains remains of successive burials from the Iron Age, a practice that apparently lasted into the 1st millennium AD. The sketch above of the burial postures of the skeletons of circle 25 shows two groups, in a staging intended to impress those attending the ceremony, who would have gathered above the ditch along the circle of monoliths. Iron spearheads placed among the corpses suggest that these collective burials took place during wartime.

The stones of the Toradja

In the Celebes (Indonesia), fields of aligned menhirs are still in use as ceremonial centers by the Toradja. Each family is a part owner of these megaliths and of the memory of the clan, ordered by genealogy and therefore symbolic of the greatness or decline of the group. Transporting and installing the largest stones (20 feet high [6 meters], 8 tons) required considerable effort, supported by sacrificial ceremonies that added to the magic of the place, as hundreds of pigs were immolated. Today the tradition endures, though the size of the stones used is far more modest (only 8 to 12 inches—20 to 30 cm—tall). The festival now involves the effigy of the deceased stationed in front of the coffin. Buffalo fights take place in the nearby rice field before the animals are slaughtered and their flesh is distributed to the participants. The celebration around the standing stones lasts all night, and between the prayers and chants a new megalith is born, raised in place among its peers.

Tombs and gods of the Americas

In the Magdalena River valley in Colombia, on terraces cut into a mountain at an altitude of some 7,000 feet (2,100 meters), megalithic tombs form a unit that is both classical and unique on the continent. Since the 6th century BC the residents of San Agustín have been building coffers of slabs for burials. These tombs then become monumental, of the passage dolmen type (above). The menhir statues placed at the entrance are clearly related to the ancient gods of Central America: the jaguar god (left), the monkey god, and the reptile god. The resemblance of these monuments to those in Europe illustrates the phenomenon of convergence. At great distances and at different periods, architectures may follow a similar evolution without any direct contact between the regions.

beings and their environment—and beyond that it suggests that Neolithic people grasped the role of the brain in human behavior. The Stone Age people who arranged their dead in megalithic monuments knew how to extract diseased teeth and sometimes even how to trepan skulls—with success, apparently, since the patient sometimes survived the ordeal.

This was proven by the first excavators, such as Baron Joseph de Baye, starting in 1872, in the hypogea of the Marne. Some trepanned skulls show bony scarred ridges attesting to the person's survival. The extracted cranial disks were made into amulets.

During the Renaissance, French surgeon Ambroise Paré had drawn attention to the difficulties of this operation—including controlling bleeding, (which is especially copious from the head), cauterization of the wound (not to mention the risk of infection), and the use of cloths drenched in vinegar to sponge up the blood and avoid putrefaction. Nevertheless, a series of skulls left in megalithic tombs near Rodez (in southern France), demonstrate the frequency of trepanning in Neolithic times.

In the passage of tumulus A in Bougon, France, a cranial section dating from 4000 BC shows three successive trepannings. For the first, a circular disk was removed at the left occiput at an angle to avoid damaging the brain; perhaps this was intended to cure pain caused by a malformation in the area. The operation seems to have succeeded, and anthropologists estimate that the patient lived some additional ten years. During that time he was operated on a second time for the removal of an oval piece of bone to increase the original opening. Perhaps the man had continued to suffer.

At the time of his death, he seems to have undergone an autopsy, a large portion of the frontal and parietal bones of the skull having been cut away with flint. The

A flint arrowhead was embedded in a human vertebra (left) found in one of the rock-cut tombs at Les Ronces at Villevenard (Marne). It was shot with the force of a bow. This death arose from a warlike act of aggression or a sacrifice. In certain ossuaries in southern France, numerous bodies were buried together, many of them bearing traces of violent death. They form a level referred to as the "death layer." Explicit signs of warlike killing become more numerous in the 3rd millennium BC, which saw the end of the building of megaliths and the advent of the age of metals.

Trepanned human skulls testify to prehistoric surgery, which developed around 4000 BC. Using flint tools, the surgeon's job was to detach a bone disk without touching the brain. Above: amulets made from cranial sections.

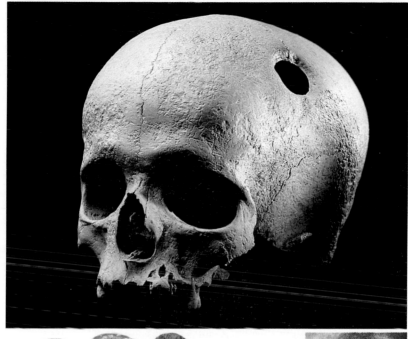

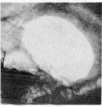

cuts were made showing no concern about protecting the cranial contents. Evidence from three other French instances of such postmortem investigation —one at Cibournios (Lozère) and two in the valley of the Petit Morin (Marne)—confirm the Neolithic experimental and scientific curiosity about the functioning of the living human body.

At that time, the same curiosity was also directed to the body after death, as we see from the ritual treatment of human bones and the numerous practices of secondary ritual during which these bones, especially the skull, attained the status of relics.

A skull from a hypogeum in the region of the Marne (photograph, top, and x-ray, above) shows clear traces of the tools used for the trepanning.

The themes of megalithic art recur in the selection of offerings placed in the tombs. One example is seen in axes with pointed handles and wide blades; such a shape is carved in one of the slabs from Gavrinis, France (left, above). Similar axes of jadeite were placed in Breton tombs (left). The blade shows no sign of use, and there is a perforation at the narrow handle end, showing that this is not a utilitarian ax but a pendant, symbolic of male power and comparable to the wooden crook and the bow (which is rarely found, although flint arrowheads indicate its presence in tombs).

Ceremonies and conventions: the respect for valuables

The offerings placed in the tombs seemed mostly to be collective, arranged, for instance, in the middle of coffers or near the threshold of the burial chamber (as in the hypogeum of Les Mournouards, in the Marne region), for all the ancestors present in the tomb. They include arrow shafts, blades, and flint nuclei (all useful objects), vases originally containing a

In the 3rd millennium BC, the ax changed shape but remained emblematic of power. Left: a small flint blade is enclosed in a sheath of antler, perforated to receive the handle. In Ireland the ax was transformed into a polished mace (two examples below) made of black stones called "hard stones." After 2000 BC the dagger replaced the ax as a symbol of power.

beverage, and especially necklace beads of variscite, limestone, and shell, along with polished axes of fibrolith, jadeite, and chloromelanite. The jadeite axes, frequent in megalithic tombs of Brittany, constituted treasures, as is shown by the seventeen axes contained in a single hiding place in Arzon (Morbihan). Petrographic studies lead to the conclusion that this

rock, prized in the Neolithic era all over Western Europe and as far away as Canterbury, originated in the Alps. Variscite (which was abundant in Brittany and in west-central France and perhaps originated in Catalonia), jadeite, and other precious stones—along with copper and gold—are the standards in a system of values that gave meaning to the ceremonies accompanying the placing of

human bones and the commemorations repeatedly performed in the vault as long as it functioned. The many eagle bones in the tomb of Isbister, in Orkney, are no doubt a rare emblem of tribal identity. Vestiges propped up in the sealed-off passage of the tombs symbolize the transition from the external world of earthly life to the funerary world of the ancestors. In front of the hidden entrance, other offerings were placed as a sign of veneration for ancestors who had become abstract entities. Many vases, identified from the seven thousand fragments found during the excavation, had been placed in front of the facade of the megalithic mound of Groenhoef at Horsens (Jutland, Denmark). To the best of our knowledge, closed and open structures oriented on the great solar axes and serving funerary functions

There were decorative elements inside the tombs beside the axes, flint spears, and other masculine symbols. Variscite beads (opposite) and rings of jadeite or serpentine were found in the megalithic tombs of Morbihan (this page). Their external diameter (4 inches, or 10 cm) makes it improbable that they served as jewelry; they are symbolic rather than utilitarian. The same applies to other bracelets of the same period, made of sculpted and polished spondyles, shells of the eastern Mediterranean that were spread around in tombs from the Black Sea as far as the Paris basin. The prestige of these objects appealed to Neolithic farmers.

(witness the alignment of Cojoux at St.-Just) were the setting for intellectualized ceremonies honoring ancestors.

The science of blood relations: key to the funerary rites?

In the megalithic gallery grave of La Chaussé-Tirancourt, France, burial cells were isolated, sometimes physically by rows of stones—as is frequently the case in the monuments of northern Germany, Scandinavia, and the Orkney Islands. There is reason to

Beads and pendants of variscite, an attractive turquoise-green stone essentially composed of phosphorus, were undoubtedly very valuable. Left: a pendant and beads found in the megalithic monument of Er Grah at Locmariaquer, France. Below: variscite beads from the megalithic tombs of Tumiac and Tuchen Pol (Ploemeur) and the Morbihan area of Brittany. These same variscite beads are also found in Portugal and Catalonia, where it is likely that they were used in prehistoric times.

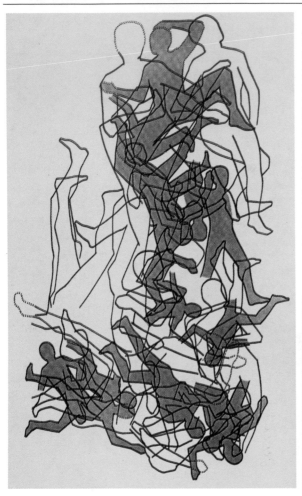

At Talheim, near Stuttgart, excavations in 1983–84 revealed collective funeral practices. Sixteen children and at least nine men and seven women were buried there around 5000 BC. Eighteen skulls bore the traces of ax blows, indicating that these people were massacred and their bodies dumped in this ditch without any particular care. Warfare probably led to the use of such mass graves, a fact that captures the reality of life at the time in that area.

believe that the bones in each of the cells belonged to members of a single family.

Starting in 1885, at Damerancourt (Oise, France), physical resemblances in bone were observed, indicating a family unit. In 1965 in the mortuary house at Niederbösa, Germany, the archaeologist Herbert Ullrich was struck by details of the skeletons that indicated two distinct population groups. Claude Masset, at La Chaussée-Tirancourt, observed three familial subgroups on the basis of "discrete" bone characteristics (supplementary suture on the skull, double feeder hole on one bone, supplementary articulating surface in a certain joint), which coincided with the distribution of bones in the physically separated cells.

These characteristics seemed to correspond with matrimonial rules of Neolithic society. Whenever a large enough sampling is available, especially in the latter period of the Neolithic, it is possible to posit an elementary parentage structure. The collective grave corresponds to an exogamous group, and each of the subgroups to endogamous units. It is too soon yet to determine whether the collective graves can provide information on the demography of this era.

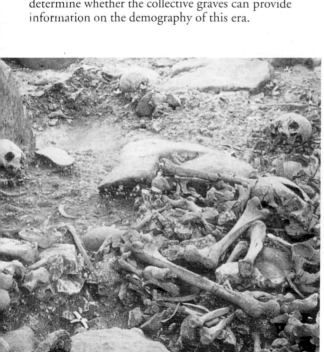

Inside the gallery grave of La Chaussée-Tirancourt, zones set off by alignments of small slabs (above) constitute symbolic burial cells that each contained the bodies or bones of the members of a single family or of a single group (left, a cell being excavated). In the foreground, at left, the skull and a few of the long bones of a single individual were gathered against the lateral slab and in the angle formed by the small slabs. Farther back, another skull was also placed against the slab. The pile of bones on the right side gives an idea of the difficulty of interpreting the sequence in which these skeletal remains were placed at the site.

In response to social hierarchization, religious aspirations, and scientific challenges, the political leaders, architects, and priests of Neolithic Europe designed and erected megalithic constructions. These monuments communicate the major currents at the heart of a great rural civilization and have left the European countryside forever transformed.

CHAPTER 5
BETWEEN HEAVEN AND EARTH

Megalithic architecture is a terrestrial and celestial marker on the landscape. Stonehenge was designed to observe the position of the sunrise at the horizon on the day of summer solstice (opposite), thus establishing the solar calendar, which regulated country work—all under the protection of the ancestors or gods sculpted into stone (right, the statue-menhir of Maurels at Calmels-et-le-Viala, Aveyron).

Choice materials for prestigious users

Contrary to common opinion, megaliths are rarely crude or unplanned. A careful observer will distinguish markings, now worn down by rainwater and frost. And even when the shape of the stone is irregular, its overall appearance shows it was selected and quarried with care. La Roche aux Fées (Fairies' Rock) at Essé, the finest dolmen in Brittany, is made of enormous blocks of red shale taken from a rock bed two and a half miles away. While fairies were carrying stones in their aprons—so the story goes—they let one stone get away, and the result is this isolated menhir.

At Stonehenge (above) bluestones were raised in the foreground, at the foot of large sarsen trilithons. Each kind of rock had a specific function. The choice of materials for sites was dictated by what was available locally.

Thus, in northern Europe dolmens were gathered from glacial moraines (left, in Sweden).

The texture and color of a stone's grain often bespeak a good knowledge of local geology. Priest-architects would have taken the best that was available in the area. In chalky earth at Bougon, the tombs' pillars match one another and are made of the local rock, from the Callovian age. The covering slabs, however, are of a different texture. One is a 32-ton block of Bathonian flint and clayey rock from an outcropping two and a half miles away, and another is a fossiliferous coralline massif weighing 90 tons that was excavated at a distance of several hundred yards.

The bluestones of Stonehenge, each weighing between 1 and 1.5 tons, form a double circle that has been incomplete since the last centuries of the 3rd millennium BC. For the most part, they are made of dolerite, though some are gray-blue volcanic lava, two are blue sandstone, and one is limestone. They were selected as much for color as for their geological quality. The chief dolerite deposit in the vicinity was found in the Prescelly Mountains in Wales, 150 miles (225 km) from Stonehenge—a distance that attests to the value placed on that type of rock. The trilithons (structures made up of two upright stones and a horizontal lintel) of Stonehenge were made of sarsen, a sandstone from Marlborough Downs, 20 miles (34 km) to the north. Because of the weight of the sarsen monoliths—they are estimated to weigh an average of 30 tons each—hauling them was a feat. In another example, the builders of Hunenbedden searched out enormous sandstone boulders from glacial moraines that were said to have been handled by giants and dwarfs. It is clear that the materials for assembling a megalithic construction were carefully chosen, and the process was governed by the function and appearance of the stone. All this shows a thorough familiarity with the geological

The choice of stones—detailed, aesthetic, and functional—reveals the funerary and sacred dimension of the megaliths. This is very much the case with the dolmen of La Roche aux Fées, or Fairies' Rock (below). The tomb was sealed and covered by the small stones of a mound, and the exterior itself became a venerated site. Even the work involved in building the chamber seems to have been a sacred act, with its own set of rules and demands. The completed artwork was dedicated to ancestors rather than to the living, who would see only the stone and earthen tumulus, not the subtleties undertaken in the work on the blocks. It is the ruined condition of the monument that reveals to us the religious purpose of the builders.

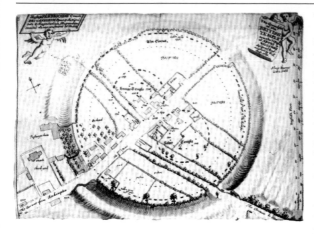

William Stukeley demonstrated the scope and complexity of Avebury and its environs (Wiltshire, England) in this drawing (opposite). The plan, left, shows the large (1,300 feet, or 397 meters across) circular levee lined with an interior ditch and then a circle of raised stones which itself surrounds two smaller circles and tangents of menhirs (which have since disappeared). Four passages placed at the cardinal points provided exits and entrances to this vast circular complex.

substratum and the shades of difference in rocks' texture and color.

Megaliths: their earthly and cosmic landscape

In around 1723 William Stukeley had the first inkling that the prehistoric monuments of Avebury and Stonehenge—megaliths, tumuli, graves, and earth mounds—were the architecture of a vast landscape complex. He set out to draw it. The topography in the pictures is well observed, while the absence of trees makes the general plan all the clearer. His drawings help us understand that the monuments were meant to be seen from afar; undoubtedly, their location was dictated by a mapmaker's point of view and a hierarchic sense of geography that can be made out only on aerial projections.

The sense of space in open megalithic architecture is very original, as demonstrated by the "avenues" at Stonehenge and Callanish and the alignments of raised stones in Carnac and St.-Just, where a straight line stretching for miles underlines the curves of the topography.

One mile from Avebury's southern gate, a double alignment of raised stones connects to the small circle of the Sanctuary, and a similar gallery leads from the north. Both are visible on the sketch below.

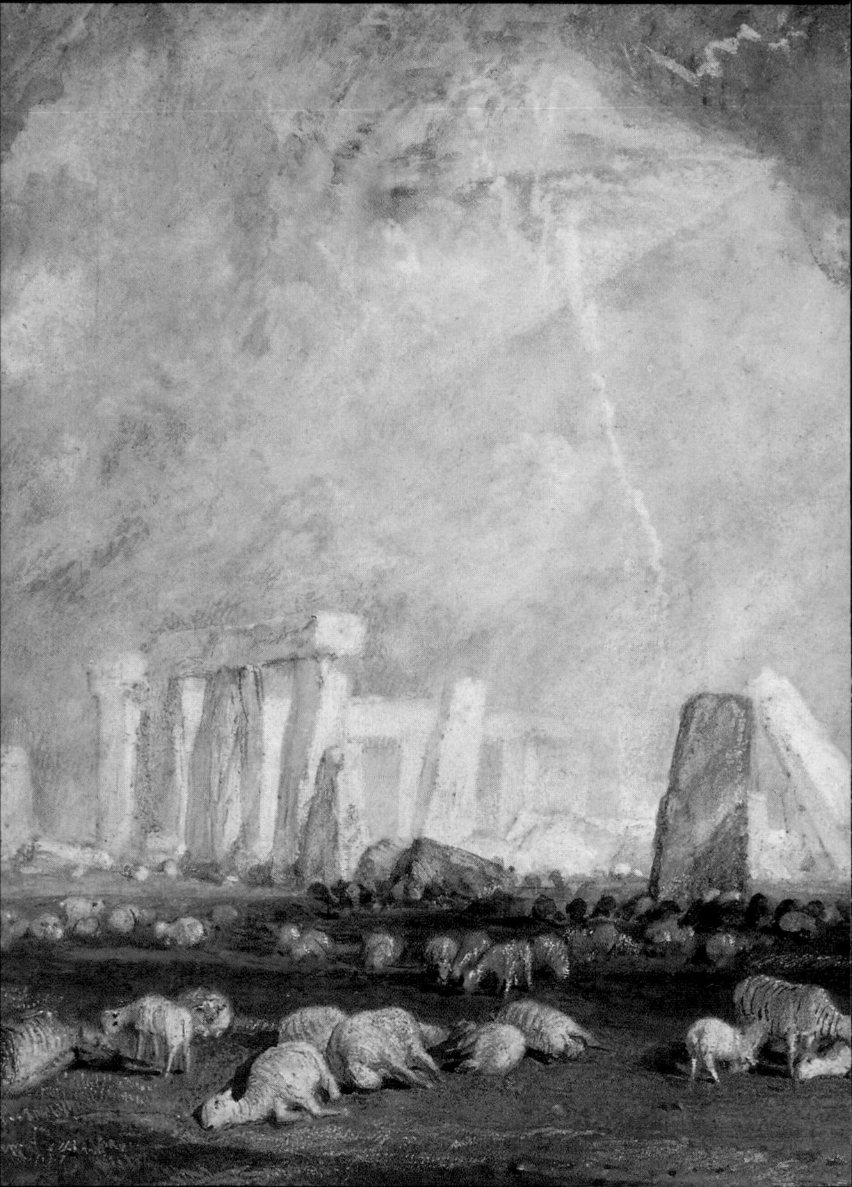

Reveries amid the ruins

The spell of the ancient ruins was one of the favorite subjects of the Romantic painters and poets. Similarly, they poured out their emotions before these megaliths, monuments that were unexplained in their time. Before a gloomy and massive megalithic tomb, amid a landscape of gnarled trees, a man—perhaps the painter Caspar David Friedrich himself—ponders the past (left). The Norwegian painter Johan Christian Dahl also painted megaliths—this one in Denmark—in a lonely setting (pages 114–15). Their English contemporaries John Constable and J. M. W. Turner were both fascinated by Stonehenge. Constable visited the site for the first time on 15 July 1820 and spent a long time reworking its image in watercolor in his studio. His view of Stonehenge with a double rainbow, which lends the monument a cosmic air, dates from 1835 (pages 108–9). Turner visited Stonehenge on several occasions and depicted it as frozen in the eternity of a pastoral landscape (pages 110–11).

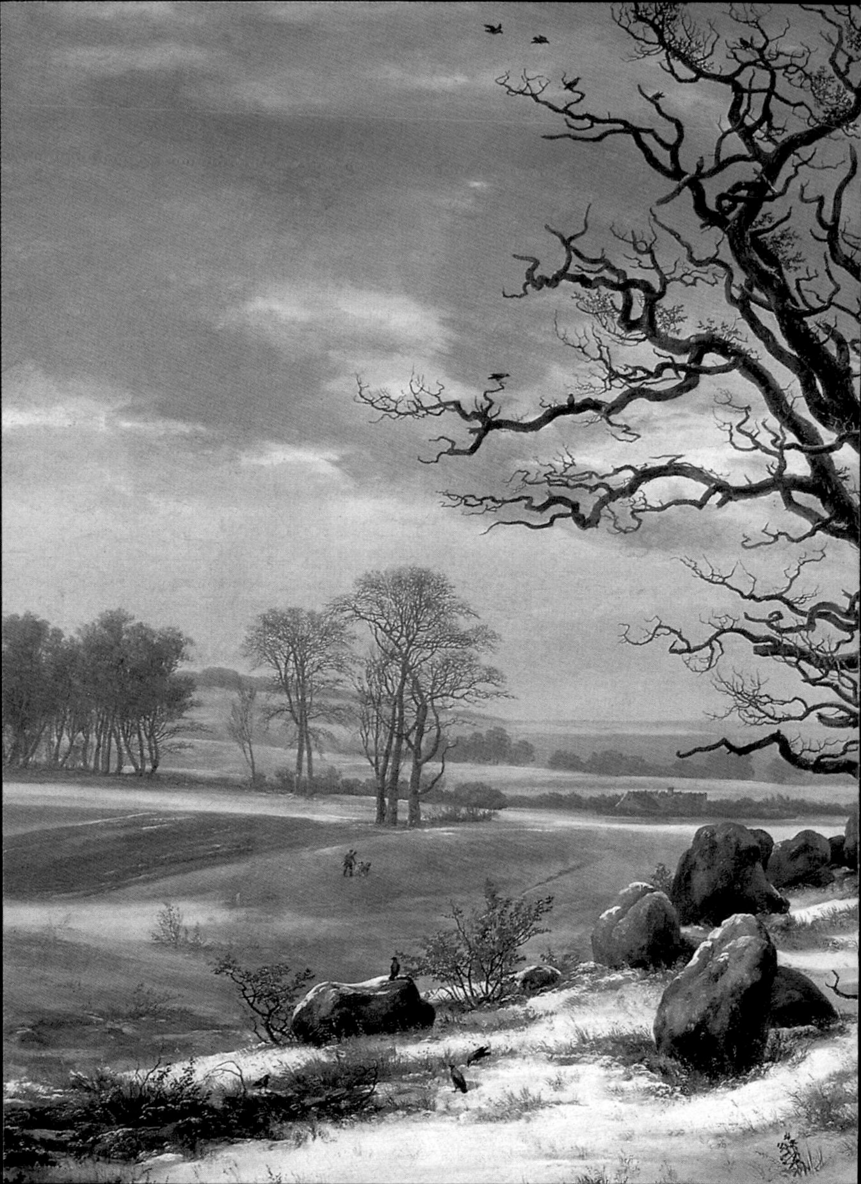

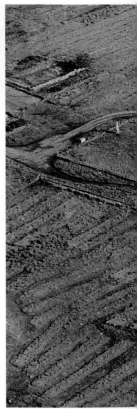

Callanish (left and below), on Lewis (the Hebrides, Scotland), was originally a modest megalithic tomb protected by a circular mound. Later it was surrounded by a circle of raised stones that led to four double alignments oriented to the cardinal axes.

Built on the peaks and sides of hills, closed constructions, such as the megalithic tombs, are at points of convergence. They stand at one end of a long line—the long axis of passage—that reaches to the point at which the sun appears at the horizon on a noteworthy day of the year. Clearly, the megalithic landscape is not just terrestrial; the modulated topography interacts with the sunlight, source of warmth and fertility. The regular path of the sun moves in tandem with that of the moon, and the observation of heavenly bodies seems to provide other reference points on the horizon in some regions, such as Scotland or England.

It is the archaeologist's job to find traces of occupation on the ground—various types of principal and secondary dwellings—and to establish their chronologies in an effort to reconstruct the history of these places and their makers. Other researchers are attracted to the sites as well. Geologists test rock outcroppings, and enthusiasts of more esoteric schools of thought come to tap the telluric currents or magnetic nodes of the place where the stones were planted.

The megalithic imagination and the great mother goddess

Enthusiasm for studying the megaliths, "megalithomania," reached its high point in the 19th century and inspired the first modern studies. The large stones captured the public imagination. In the distant past, people had connected architecture, science, and religion, invoking as witness the great motion of celestial bodies in the skies, through the brilliant innovation of the megaliths. With new multidisciplinary methods of study, the intentions inscribed in the stones are becoming increasingly accessible to us. The modern imagination,

The evolution of Callanish seems typical for the British Isles. The megalithic tomb passage remains a reference to a monument with open design tied to solar and, no doubt, lunar observation, as at Stonehenge. Other stone circles in Scotland were designed as lunar observatories.

poring over these mythic beginnings of art and science, thus meets up with ancient intention. Everyone is engaged in this quest. Urban culture hopes to find the meaning of landscape messages; rural culture would like to refine its knowledge of history and archaeology.

Integrated into their landscape, megaliths are the monumental witnesses of this consciousness of a fundamental and sacred ecology. Many seem dominated by a female figure, whom Jacques Cauvin identifies as the Neolithic divinity—an omnipresent mother goddess who takes the form of graven idols, sculptures, and statue-menhirs. A warrior god is her counterpart, represented merely by the image of his arms, ax, crook, and bow in the Neolithic period, and by a dagger from the Chalcolithic age (3rd millennium BC).

The challenge of the Neolithic

The impressive megalithic creations of the West—raised stones or burial stones under tumuli—inevitably pose the problem of their construction. We may suppose that there had to be a determined and diplomatic chief to assemble troops capable of moving such slabs; and the task also required geological engineers, who knew where to find good stone and how to move and install the giant blocks—truly a remarkable feat. No doubt a religious authority also was needed to determine the placement and direction of the monument and to confer its ultimate purpose as a tomb for ancestral relics or a center of ceremony.

How megaliths were moved and raised using Neolithic technology has long been a mystery, giving birth to the most extravagant theories. Various

The anthropomorphic statue of Catel, in Guernsey, with very stylized shoulders and head, can be identified as a Neolithic mother goddess because of the remaining breast surmounted by a necklace and the position of the arms and hands (clasped in the manner of Near Eastern goddesses). The face is not sculpted; perhaps it was once painted.

people have suggested the use of hydraulic locks, conveyor belts made of grass and logs, or slides on frozen ground, extraterrestrial intervention, or telluric or magnetic force—modern-day versions of yesteryear's titans. To put such hypotheses to rest, several have been tested in the field.

Dug into the chalk wall of the hypogeum of Razet à Coizard (Marne), this mother goddess is identified by her breasts and the necklace holding a large pearl.

At Stonehenge Richard Atkinson had his students try to haul some slabs; the strength of thirty-two students was required to move one 1.5-ton block. In July 1979—on a plateau in Chaumes, Exoudun, the location of the rock bed that was the source for the 32-ton slab used in the Bougon tomb at Deux-Sèvres—a block of the same weight was hauled by two hundred people and then raised by sixty, using three large levers and period tools: wooden rollers, braided plant fiber, polished axes to cut tree trunks, antler picks and wooden wedges to cut the rock, and flint

The experiment carried out in 1979 in Bougon demonstrated that two hundred people could haul a 32-ton block (below). The block was placed on rollers set on wooden rails. While some people pulled, others used small levers to assure that the blocks moved in a straight line; some in the back pushed

or pulled as necessary. Bernard Poissonnier succeeded in moving the same enormous block with only a few dozen people, who used levers attached to each roller, making the block shift more easily (opposite, above).

hammers to shape it. The technique was improved in 1997 with a hub-and-spokes system.

We are left with no doubt that megalithic mechanics were remarkably sophisticated. There is no way for us to know exactly what method was used to construct the monuments, but we can be sure that it was possible for humans to do this work. To handle the weight of the stones, however, they had to be masters of engineering concepts of such complexity that their skills may be compared to those of the greatest architects.

Megalithic measurement and geometry: empirical rationalism

At the beginning of the 20th century, the engineer A. Kerviler was intrigued by the fairly regular increments of distance that existed between the menhirs at Carnac and some other sites. He proposed

standards of prehistoric measurement: the megalithic foot (1 foot, or 0.30 meter), the megalithic pace (3 feet, or 0.90 meter), and the megalithic cord (30 paces, 90 feet, or 27 meters). A professor of engineering at Oxford took up the theory and measured the distances between hundreds of raised stones in the

Thinking of the Egyptians, who used the Nile to transport rafts of stones for the pyramids and colossal temples, some archaeologists believe that stones from far away like those at Stonehenge, came by sea and then by river. To transport a 1.5-ton block, the equivalent of a Stonehenge bluestone, archaeologist Richard Atkinson linked three flat-bottomed boats that were each fitted out with rolling logs on which the block was placed (thus allowing it to be easily moved onto land). Four of Atkinson's students conducted this experiment (left).

British Isles and in Brittany. In common English, he defined the megalithic yard (3 feet, or 0.899 meter, corresponding to Kerviler's "pace") and the megalithic rod (2.5 yards, or 2.07 meters).

Using these precise figures, in the 1960s the researcher Alexander Thom observed constructions of simple, semicircular figures built from right-angle triangles on a Pythagorean ratio of 3, 4, and 5. In 1977 he described the geometry of the alignments of Carnac, with the megalithic yard as the standard of measurement. Thom demonstrated the importance of the large menhir of the Manio tumulus and the Great Broken Menhir of Locmariaquer and

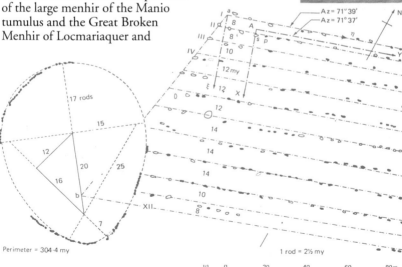

claimed they were both reference points for solar and lunar observations. If recent excavations at Locmariaquer no longer yield such

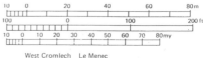

West Cromlech   Le Menec

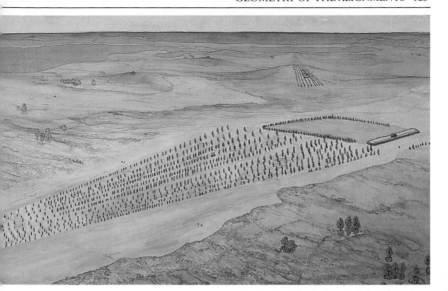

decisive conclusions—because the large menhir turns out in fact not to have been isolated—archaeologists still are interested in Thom's approach and his other work as well. In Scotland he was able to study the two hundred raised stones of Mid Clyth, fanning out in a north-south direction, and single or double rows of menhirs extending for miles from east to west, as in Eleven Sheares and Rhos y Beddan. Similar stone alignments are found in Cornwall, and Dartmoor (southern England).

Stone circles, which are numerous in the British Isles, were studied by A. Burl in 1976. One of these complexes, integrated into the landscape of Mainland Island in the Orkneys, serves a double function—it had a funerary purpose, and it was also an observatory for the stars. It comprises two circles next to the large megalithic tomb of Maes Howe. The first is composed of the twelve Stones of Stenness in a channel interrupted by an entranceway leading to a central funerary coffer; the second circle, called the Ring of Brodgar, is 350 feet across (107 meters) and is made of sixty stones bordering a channel dug out of red sandstone.

Using data gathered by the Scientific Imaging Service at the University of Bordeaux, Jean-Claude Golvin created these reconstructions of the large complexes of Carnac (above and opposite above). These panoramic views of the alignments of Kermario and Kerlescan were created on a computer.

Alexander Thom's diagrams (opposite below) show the geometric construction of the alignments of Le Ménec in Carnac.

The megaliths, the sun, and the moon: the logic of cycles

Two monuments—Callanish (on Lewis, an island in the Outer Hebrides) and above all Stonehenge, the most revealing—exemplify how a megalithic observatory of the sun's course functioned. In 1666 John Aubrey identified Stonehenge as a temple and discovered the circle with fifty-six holes, each 2.5 to 6 feet (.8 to 1.8 meters) in diameter (today they are filled in), that bordered the embankment. This ridge was lined with a circular channel that was broken at the northeast by the beginning of the "avenue," oriented toward the point of the rising sun on the day of summer solstice. This direction is confirmed by the Heel Stone, a 20-foot-high (6 meters) sarsen megalith, which was placed in the direct line of sight for

In its first phase, at the end of the 4th millennium BC, the site of Stonehenge on Salisbury Plain seems unextraordinary—it is a simple circular ditch surrounded by a bank. At the end of this first phase, the entrance of the site and the Heel Stone were put up (below). In the second phase, three to five centuries later, the fifty-six holes known as "Aubrey Holes" were dug (opposite, 1). During the third phase, around the end of the 3rd millennium BC, the bluestones were raised in the center of the site (2); the avenue confirms the privileged positioning of the site, namely, toward the point on the horizon where the sun rises on the summer solstice. The sarsen trilithons would have been put up during a fourth phase (3) at the beginning of the Bronze Age.

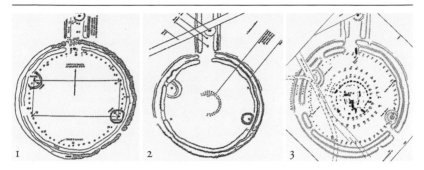

an observer standing exactly in the middle of the circle. This first layout is linked to the phase called Stonehenge I, which must have been a bit before 3000 BC.

According to Gerald Hawkins (American astrophysicist and author of the celebrated and controversial *Stonehenge Decoded*, 1965), a rectangle inscribed in the initial circle—from four post holes, two of which are surrounded by a little trough—was needed to establish the position of the viewer for optimal observation of the sun and, as it turned out, the moon. He showed that the monuments functioned as an instrument able to chart solar and lunar movements. The solar and lunar cycles would intersect, and eclipses in particular could be predicted. The later improvements at Stonehenge (phases II, III, IV) are more spectacular in that they include the central crown of three trilithons within the sarsen "horseshoe" as well as the circle of bluestones. The sole aim of these improvements—which were undertaken until approximately 1500 BC—

The center of the circular monument at Stonehenge could be said to be the ideal point for solar and lunar observation, the basis for an actual astronomical geometry.

was to realize the initial astronomical purpose.

Orientation toward the sun, particularly in relation to sunrise, is common in megalithic structures, especially along the axis of the grave passage (at Gavrinis and Newgrange, for example). Lunar observation is attested to by circles of raised stones in Scotland, where the purpose of the stone altar, or recumbent stone, southwest of the monument was to observe the course of the moon.

Survival and renaissance of the megaliths

Aside from their efforts to learn the methods of construction, the ceremonial functions, and the ancient environmental integration of the megalithic monuments, public authorities work with archaeologists, architects, and landscapers to protect the physical and spiritual integrity of these constructions in the modern world. One man, Michael J. O'Kelly, pursued these goals to the point of reconstructing Newgrange, including its two-color facade of white quartz and black granite pebbles. With its ornate and unusual surrounding rocks and its tomb, the monument has become one of Ireland's proudest symbols. It is more difficult to reconcile Stonehenge with our modern, sensation-hungry world. On the summer solstice, the site attracts many people who seek harmony with nature.

How can Stonehenge be protected from crowds?

Tomorrow maybe too late.
Rescue

Threats to the monuments have increased as highways, rail lines, and airports have been constructed. This English poster depicting a bulldozer removing the complex of trilithons from Stonehenge points out the risks of development near the archaeological sites.

Other reinforcements and modes of presentation have been undertaken at Knowth in Ireland, at Barnenez and Bougon in France, and at Hal Saflieni in Malta. Carnac and Locmariaquer are certainly objects of study, but determining how to display them is not simple. There is a conflict between the vulnerability of the monuments and their natural environment, and the demands of a growing mass tourism attracted to the uniqueness of the sites. The preservation of these constructions will not occur through the resurrection of the Neolithic period, which is lost forever, but only through integrating protection and watchful respect for its cultural heritage into our way of thinking and our culture.

After being explored and excavated by Michael O'Kelly, the tumulus covering the megalithic tomb of Newgrange was reinforced and its facade was reconstructed as it must have appeared in the Neolithic period (above). This restoration protects the original parts of the monument, allowing visitors access to the central tomb, and furthers an understanding of the monument's function.

Stones of memory, the megaliths are an ancient testament to Europe's past. Stonehenge itself epitomizes the unique character of these monuments and symbolizes the legacy of Neolithic people. Its image will never exhaust its power (left, the final frame from the film *Tess*, directed by Roman Polanski, and overleaf).

DOCUMENTS

The centuries passed. The remote descendants of the disinherited builders have assumed an all-but-unlimited power. They can read these stones, nothing but stones left straight up in the ground, which their disconcerted learning labels with a Greek term, the earliest testimony of a dark ambition, their own, as excessive, as poorly restrained and as solitary as the stones themselves.

And they marvel that these deformed steles inaugurate the whole history of their species.

Roger Caillois,
Pierres suivi d'autres textes
(Stones, Followed by Other Texts),
Paris, 1966

Sacred Stonehenge

English antiquarian and physician William Stukeley (1687–1765) stressed the architectural and religious aspects of this extraordinary ancient monument. His strong views about Stonehenge shaped the theories of several generations of thinkers.

Who built Stonehenge?

Tho' Stonehenge be the proudest singularity of this sort, in the world, as far as we know: yet there are so many others, manifestly form'd upon the same, or kindred design, by the same measure, and for the same purpose, all over the Britan[n]ic isles; that we can have no room to doubt of their being made by the same people, and that by direction of the British Druids.

There are innumerable, from the land's end in Cornwall, to the utmost northern promontory in Scotland, where the Roman power never reach'd. They are to be found in all the islands between Scotland and Ireland, isle of Man, all the Orkney islands, &c. and numerous in Ireland itself.

And there is no pretence, as far as I

Previous page: the alignment of Kermario at Carnac.

Avebury, as depicted in Stukeley's 1743 book on the site.

View of the Cell of the Celtic Temple at Albury. Aug. 16. 1721

The Cove of the Northern temple.

can see, for any other persons or nations being the founders of them. They are circles of stones, generally rude, of different diameters, upon elevated ground, barren, open heaths and downs; chiefly made of stones taken from the surface of the ground.

Celtic monuments, from Stukeley's *Itinerarum Curiosum*, 1724.

There are no remembrances of the founders, any other than an uninterrupted tradition of their being sacred, that there is medicinal value in them; that they were made by the Irish; that they were brought from Afric[a]; that they were high-places of worship; sanctuaries; bowing, adoring places; and what names they commonly have,

Stukeley's influential book on Stonehenge contained many depictions of the site.

intimate the same thing. And in many places the express remembrance and name of Druids remain, and the people bury their dead in or near them to this day, thinking them holy ground....

Whatever is dug up at or near these works are manifestly remains of the Druid times; urns, bones, ornaments of amber, glass beads, snake stones, amulets, celts, flint-hatchets, arrowheads and such things as bespeak the rudest ages, the utmost antiquity, most early plantations of people that came into our island soon after Noah's flood.

I have all the reason in the world to believe them an oriental colony of Phoenicians; at least that such a one came upon the first Celtic plantation of people here.

William Stukeley,
*Stonehenge, A Temple Restor'd
to the British Druids,*
1740

On the meaning of the dolmens

Christophe Paul de Robien (1698–1756), an official in Brittany, was the first to reject the romantic notions that megaliths had served as the site for human sacrifice. He understood their function as burial sites, a view that came to prevail by the turn of the 20th century, following the first modern comparative ethnographic studies.

Dolmens were said to have magical powers and have long been the site of various mystical celebrations.

On the Gallic tombs

The tombs are formed of stones of immense dimensions borne on other stones raised to a standing position to sustain them.… We know that the Gauls always buried their dead outside the walls of their habitations and built tombs of this kind for them. These stones, so striking in their grandeur that we can scarcely believe they are human handiwork, are less astonishing when we consider the prodigious size of the pyramids used by the Egyptians to hold their dead. The Gauls and other northern peoples, less refined but no less religious, had diverse means of making up for what they lacked in the way of artistry and magnificence. The whole western coast of Brittany is filled with their monuments, as is northern Europe, and if so many had not been destroyed, they might be infinite in their multitude.

Christophe Paul de Robien,
Description historique et topographique de l'ancienne Armorique
(Historical and Topographical Description of Ancient Armorica), manuscript preserved in the library of Rennes, France, 1698–1756

A Druidic altar

At some distance from Carnac, Brittany, between Locmariaquer and the woods of Kérantré, we find a Druidic altar whose table is supported on three enormous stone fragments.

Diodorus of Sicily says that the Gauls swore to their treaties on such altars, where art and nature made peace; and here the Druids, their priests, made sacrifices to the gods, most often choosing humans as their victims. The enormous stone that covers this monument is called, in our language, dolmen.

Théophile de La Tour d'Auvergne,
Les Origines gauloises
(The Origins of the Gauls),
1796

A sacrificial monument

The permanent altars, in raw stone, were these Celtic monuments that archaeologists call dolmens, altars that must have been built in pure stone, untouched by iron, for its contact would have polluted them. The table of the dolmens was the site on which offerings were made of sacrificial beasts, and all too often it was stained with the blood of human victims. After the immolation and cremation of the victim, it was also on this altar that one consumed the portion of these victims reserved as food for those who offered them and for the priests who had this right.

Henry,
"On the origin of the monuments of raw stone,"
Revue archéologique, 1850

Simple funerary monuments

The purpose of the dolmens leaves no further doubt today. Barely a score of years ago it was still possible to see them as altars erected for human sacrifice; the earth had not yet uncovered these monuments, and the free-ranging imagination of archaeologists could indulge itself in seeking to confirm the theories of their day; but since then so many explorations have revealed in these monuments the presence of skeletons, or at least the clear evidence of graves. There can be no further doubt: dolmens and tumuli are funeral

monuments. As for the supposed corners occupied by victims' corpses, and the channels intended to catch their blood, it seems proven fact today that they had no reality other than in the imagination of the antiquarian scholars of yesterday.… If there were need of further proof to convince our readers of their funerary origins, we would invoke some of the most significant names attached to these monuments. One of these, Locmaria-quer, is called the Tomb of the Ancient Man, Bé-er-gouss or Bergouss. A field at St.-Gildas-de-Rhuys, containing a gallery grave, bears the name the Field of the Tomb. At Cléguérec, a pathway leading to a dolmen is known as the Path of the Tomb. We can only conclude, then, that the dolmens are graves.

Abbé Hamard,
preface to James Fergusson's *Rude Stone Monuments of All Countries Throughout the World*,
1872

Dolmens in India

Having learned from a friend of mine who spent more than twenty years in India that megalithic monuments existed in that country, I wrote to him requesting further information, to which he answered as follows: "Dolmens are still used everywhere to reunite the remnants of families, or sometimes a whole tribe, in one place. The absolutely primitive condition of these peoples lends a special interest to their customs as well as their monuments."

Jenkyn-Jones,
"Dolmens and menhirs in the mountains of Khasia,"
Bulletin de la Société archéologique
(Bulletin of the Archaeological Society)

"The stones of Carnac are big stones!"

French novelist Gustave Flaubert (1821–1880) was curious about the megaliths, and he asked hard questions about them during a trip to Brittany. While he may have enjoyed his visit, he disdained the excesses of the Celtic-mad archaeologists of his time. His ironic commentary makes particularly good reading.

The plain of Carnac is a wide space in the countryside, on which are found eleven rows of black stones, aligned at symmetric intervals, diminishing in size the farther they are from the sea. Cambry claims there had been four thousand, and Fréminville counted twelve hundred. All we can say for sure is that they are numerous.

What was the point of all this? Are they tombs? Was this a temple? One day St. Cornille, pursued on the shore by soldiers and about to be swallowed up by the waves, imagined he could change his pursuers into stones, and indeed they were petrified. But this account satisfied none but fools, small children, and poets. Another explanation had to be found.

In the 16th century Olaus Magnus, archbishop of Uppsala (who, exiled to

Fréminville, who counted 1200 megaliths at the Carnac, depicted it in this lithograph.

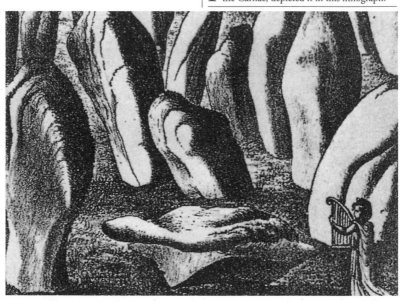

Rome, wrote a book on the antiquities of his homeland that was highly regarded everywhere, except in Sweden itself, where he obtained no translator), discovered that "when the stones form a single long, straight line, it means that underneath there lie warriors killed in duels; while stones arranged in a square are devoted to heroes who perished in battle; and those laid out in a circle are family graves, while those grouped in a corner or on an angle arrangement are the tombs of *horsemen, or even foot soldiers, especially those on the winning side.*" All that is very fine; but Olaus Magnus forgot to tell us how we are to go about burying two cousins who have killed one another in a duel, on horseback. The duel meant that the stones had to be straight; the family tomb demanded a circular arrangement; but since these were horsemen, they were to be grouped in a corner, although this was not a rigid requirement, as this system applied "especially to those on the winning side."

According to a certain Dr. Borlase, an Englishman who had observed similar stones in Cornwall, "Soldiers had been buried there at the very spot where they perished"; as if, normally, they would have been carted off to the graveyard! And he bases his theory on this comparison: "their graves are arranged in a straight line like the front of an army, in the plains that were the theater of some great exploit."

Then it's off to find the Greeks, the Egyptians, and the Indo-Chinese! There is a Carnac in Egypt, someone must have concluded, and there's one in lower Brittany. Thus it is probable that our local Karnac is a descendant of their Carnac over there. No doubt about it! Because over there, they are sphinxes,

and here stone blocks; on both coasts it's stone, whence we see that the Egyptians (a people who did not travel) came to these coasts (of which they had never heard), founded a colony here (because they founded none anywhere else), and that they must have left these rough statues (these makers of fine ones), a positive testimony to their presence here (which is mentioned by no one).

Lovers of mythology have seen these as the pillars of Hercules; lovers of natural history consider them a representation of the serpent Python because, according to Pausanias, a pile of stones like this on the road from Thebes to Elissonte was called the Serpent's Head, "all the more because the alignments of Carnac describe sinuous lines like those of a snake." The lovers of cosmography have seen a zodiac here, such as M. de Cambry, who saw in these eleven rows of stones the twelve signs of the zodiac, "for it must be said," he adds, "that the ancient Gauls had only eleven signs in their zodiac." Next, a member of the Institute has conjectured "that this could very well have been the cemetery of the Venetians" who resided at Vannes, six leagues from there, and founded Venice, as everyone knows. Another has written that these good Venetians, conquered by Caesar, raised up all these blocks, entirely in the spirit of humility and to honor Caesar. But people tired of the cemetery, the serpent, and the zodiac; they set out on a quest, and found a Druidic temple.

The few documents we have, scattered in Pliny and in Dio Cassius, agree in stating that: the Druids chose for their ceremonies dark places, the depths of woods "and their vast silence." Thus, as Carnac is beside the sea, in a sterile landscape, where nothing has ever grown but the conjectures of these

Prosper Mérimée included a field of stones in his illustration.

gentlemen, the first grenadier of France, who I doubt was the country's leading wit, followed by Pelloutier and by M. Mahé (canon of the cathedral of Vannes), concluded "that this was a temple of the Druids, in which political assemblies must also have been held."

But that was not the end of it, no, it was necessary to demonstrate to some extent the purpose empty spaces served in these alignments. "Let us discover the reason, something no one has attempted before," M. Mahé proclaimed; and, relying on a sentence by Pomponius Mela: "The Druids teach many things to the nobility, whom they instruct secretly in the remote caverns and forests" and on this comment from Lucan: "You live in high forests," he established consequently that the Druids not only serviced the sanctuaries but took up residence in them and taught school there: "Whereas, then, the monument of Carnac is a sanctuary as were the Gallic forests, there is reason to believe that the empty intervals interrupting the lines of stones must have contained rows of houses, where the Druids lived with their families and their many pupils, and in which the principals of the nation, who betook themselves to the sanctuary on days of great solemnity, found lodgings prepared for them." Good Druids! excellent churchmen! how they have been calumnied! They who lived there, so virtuously, with their family and their many pupils, and who took their amiability to the point of preparing lodgings for the principals of the nation!

But a man, at last, a man has come, imbued with the genius of things antique and disdainful of the beaten paths.

He, he alone could distinguish the remains of a Roman camp, and more precisely of a camp of Caesar's, who had raised up these stones only *to serve as a support for the soldiers' tents and to prevent their being borne off by the wind.* What tempests there must have been in days of old on the coasts of Armorica [Brittany]!

The kindly scribe who discovered, for the glory of the great Julius, this

The sum total of all these kindnesses constitutes what we know as CELTIC ARCHAEOLOGY....

To return now to the stones of Carnac (or rather to leave them), if anyone ask me, after so many opinions, which is my own, I shall utter one that is irrefutable, irrebuttable, irresistible, an opinion that would drive back the tents of M. de La Sauvagère and strike the Egyptian Penhoët with pallor, which

A 19th-century French lithograph of a Gallic execution.

sublime precaution (thus rendering unto Caesar what had never been his), was a former pupil of the Polytechnic Institute, a captain of the engineers, monsieur de La Sauvagère!

would shatter Cambry's zodiac and chop up the serpent Python in a thousand pieces. And here is that opinion: the stones of Carnac are indeed big stones!

Gustave Flaubert,
"On the stones of Carnac and Celtic archaeology,"
L'Artiste, 18 April 1858

The great journey of the megaliths

At the turn of the century, Brittany was in turmoil about its archaeological sites. First a dolmen was taken away, and then they came for the region's finest menhir! The press tells the story of both matters.

It was a curious, unexpected incident: in 1896 a man named Charles Piketty purchased a dolmen from Kerran and carried it off as an ornament for his family tomb at the cemetery of Meudon.

A perfectly legal move

Some good friends of the megalithic monuments of our old Brittany have written me a letter of warning that I can only summarize here, without incriminating anyone, since the owner of a dolmen not acquired by the State is free to sell it to anyone he chooses, even to cover the ashes of a modest pensioner in Meudon.

Well, then, a dolmen from Locmariaquer is en route at this moment to the cemetery of Meudon, where it will be placed over a family crypt as a funerary monument! No one has said whether it will have a Latin or Celtic inscription.

This dolmen is from Kerran, the town of St.-Philibert. It is made of large slabs and composed of thirteen blocks of granite, one of which bears a sculpted ax, an emblem unknown to local architects to this day. The table alone weighs 13,200 pounds. It has been placed on supports five feet high.

Without the benefit of goat or crane, this table has been transported on a platform on rollers by means of levers and jacks. Then seven men, with a triple hoist, moved it to the highway some 700 feet (213 meters) distant. It was taken to the station on a cart

The Piketty family tomb in the Meudon cemetery.

brought from Paris, drawn by sixteen horses. The expedition took place on 20 January, starting at the Auray train station, and going to the one at Les Moulineaux (Seine-et-Oise). Alert—to lovers of dolmens who are traveling. A dolmen is about to be unpacked in Meudon!

There is no accounting for taste, and everyone is free to prepare the tomb he likes. But I can't help regretting that the archaeologist from Meudon—who seems comfortable enough, to judge by the transport costs—did not leave behind the dolmen of Ker-Han…at Ker-Han and simply have his architect construct a copy at Meudon.

Moving the dolmen to its new home.

Le Petit journal,
23 January 1896

The Celtic tomb of Ker-Han

Under the title "A Celtic tomb on the road," *Le Petit Journal* recently reported that a dolmen from Locmariaquer was about to be acquired by a resident of Meudon as an ornament for a grave in the town cemetery.…

We were curious to know who had acquired this dolmen and to what tomb it was going.… [It turns out that] this dolmen is intended to decorate the tomb of M. Piketty, a rich industrialist who died about one year ago.

In his lifetime M. Piketty was both passionate and distinguished as an architect. As the correspondent of several learned societies, he was responsible for numerous archaeological discoveries of great interest carried out in the river bed of the Seine. Thanks to his great wealth, as well as his great efforts, his patience, and some degree of sacrifice, he had succeeded in amassing, in his villa on Avenue des Fauvettes in Meudon, a nearly unique collection of archaeological specimens which is now the property of his son, M. Charles Piketty, an engineer. On several occasions, then, M. Piketty Senior, in the course of conversations with friends and scholars, had expressed the wish to go to his eternal rest under one of these mysterious dolmens that he had always admired. Therefore it was to comply with his father's often expressed desires that M. Charles Piketty, in an act of filial piety, became the owner of the dolmen of Ker-Han.

A true scientific curiosity, this dolmen stands today at the entrance of the cemetery of Meudon, where it occupies an area of about 160 square feet (49 meters). The site had to be reinforced to be able to accommodate this Druidic monument, whose total weight is about 20 tons. And that, in all its simplicity, is the story of the Celtic tomb that will have, at least in comparison to most graves, the unquestionable advantage of avoiding the banal.

Le Petit journal,
29 February 1896

The Great Broken Menhir moved to Paris, side by side with the Eiffel Tower? It might have happened at the 1900 World's Fair if not for the sharp protests from Bretons.

A local newspaper takes a stand

Around the middle of the month, a letter signed by Admiral and Count Réveillère and addressed to the director of the 1900 World's Fair was published in newspapers, demanding that the exposition include the Great Broken Menhir of Locmariaquer. Soon thereafter the admiral received the response that his plan would be submitted to the World's Fair committee, and commentary on the subject, largely favorable, appeared in the press.

I admit that I was astounded, and the explanations offered in various newspapers by Admiral Réveillère did nothing to dissipate this reaction. A menhir at the World's Fair! I had to re-read the report, but could not deny the facts. I decided then that *Le Clocher breton* was duty bound to lodge a protest.
Le Clocher breton
November 1897

Response from Admiral Réveillère

Celtism is the invincible sympathy that unites the most idiosyncratic, purest, and best-preserved representatives of the remnants of that Celtic domination that extended, across a span too narrow for such a length, from Ireland to Asia Minor. Foremost among such representatives are Scotland, Ireland, Wales, and Brittany, or Armorica. They seem almost to form a utopia. Why is this? In any case, it was a challenge accepted. Any attempt to bring people together, wherever they find themselves, and whatever their nature, is a sacred undertaking.... This was the idea that

prompted us to request the removal of the menhir of Locmariaquer to Paris and its reconditioning for the 1900 World's Fair. The French press, disconcerted by this unexpected intention, felt in some vague way that this simple removal of a stone represented some strong, secret plan. The press was at a loss about how to react to a proposal championed by such partisans of Celtism as Messieurs Le Braz and Le Goffic....

The proposed transfer of the menhir of Locmariaquer to Paris divided Brittany into two camps: politics, after all, crops up everywhere and anywhere. At the bottom there lay the conflict between the Republic one and indivisible and the particularism of Brittany. This province is striving to imitate the particularism of Provence, though without any sign of success. Because, despite all traditionalists, Brittany is French to its fingertips. A lady who is part of the Breton aristocracy told me, on

The Great Broken Menhir, at home in Locmariaquer.

the subject: "I am fighting your project because I am Breton before I am French." That's the debate, in a nutshell.

"Only in Paris will it [the menhir] have symbolic value," was M. Le Goffic's forceful comment.

Indeed, it will symbolize the spiritual union of all the Megaliths, a spiritual union that weighs oddly on all the world's destinies.

Lying on the ground, on a grassy knoll in the land of Morbihan, the menhir was the symbol of a past that was venerable but irrevocably dead. Therefore the fanatical devotees of the past rebel at the idea of a transfer that would transpose it into a symbol of progress and of the future. These superstitious defenders of the old customs were joined by the poets who, to preserve the thorns rather than see a fertile soil nourishing humans, would favor a land overrun with rabbits. These medievalists commented: "The poor menhir will be homesick for the thorns." This is the very attitude that blocks avenues of communication, opposes the building of bridges, and favors the removal of regional railroads between major centers in order to avoid the spread of disease.

Rear Admiral Réveillère,
Mégalithisme, Paris, 1900

The voice of a Breton poet

Like a riddle, deep in the Quaternary Era,
long before earth knew the Sphinx of vacant gaze,
the Primitives had raised up this giant rock
that lies in four fragments, thunderstruck....

Come, awake! Paris waits: be proud!
O witness of the Flood, Ancestor of History,
go, sidle up to the Eiffel Tower, find your petty glory.
Granite colossus beside the Tower of iron,
the most surprised of all, amid the Carnival,
will be the Giant of Locmariaquer.

Frédéric Le Guyader

Tess of the d'Urbervilles

Written in 1891 by English novelist Thomas Hardy (1840–1928), Tess of the d'Urbervilles *tells of a young woman's struggle against her fate. At the end of the novel, accompanied by her beloved Angel Clare, she sinks down to rest on a fallen monolith at Stonehenge, the pagan temple of sacrifice that echoes her revolt against contemporary society.*

Though the sky was dense with cloud a diffused light from some fragment of a moon had hitherto helped them a little. But the moon had now sunk, the clouds seemed to settle almost on their heads, and the night grew as dark as a cave. However, they found their way along, keeping as much on the turf as possible that their tread might not resound, which it was easy to do, there being no hedge or fence of any kind. All around was open loneliness and black solitude, over which a stiff breeze blew.

They had proceeded thus gropingly two or three miles further when on a sudden Clare became conscious of some vast erection close in his front, rising sheer from the grass. They had almost struck themselves against it.

"What monstrous place is this?" said Angel.

"It hums," says she. "Hearken!"

He listened. The wind, playing upon

S cenes from *Tess,* the 1979 film adaptation of the Thomas Hardy novel directed by Roman Polanski.

the edifice, produced a booming tune, like the note of some gigantic one-stringed harp. No other sound came from it, and lifting his hand and advancing a step or two, Clare felt the vertical surface of the structure. It seemed to be of solid stone, without joint or moulding. Carrying his fingers onward he found that what he had come in contact with was a colossal rectangular pillar; by stretching out his left hand he could feel a similar one adjoining. At an indefinite height overhead something made the black sky blacker, which had the semblance of a vast architrave uniting the pillars horizontally. They carefully entered beneath and between; the surfaces echoed their soft rustle; but they seemed to be still out of doors. The place was roofless. Tess drew her breath fearfully, and Angel, perplexed, said—

"What can it be?"

Feeling sideways they encountered another tower-like pillar, square and uncompromising as the first; beyond it another and another. The place was all doors and pillars, some connected above by continuous architraves.

"A very Temple of the Winds," he said.

The next pillar was isolated; others composed a trilithon; others were prostrate, their flanks forming a causeway wide enough for a carriage; and it was soon obvious that they made up a forest of monoliths grouped upon the grassy expanse of the plain. The couple advanced further into this pavilion of the night till they stood in its midst.

"It is Stonehenge!" said Clare.

"The heathen temple, you mean?"

"Yes. Older than the centuries; older than the d'Urbervilles! Well, what shall we do, darling? We may find shelter further on."

But Tess, really tired by this time, flung herself upon an oblong slab that lay close at hand, and was sheltered from the wind by a pillar. Owing to the action of the sun during the preceding day the stone was warm and dry, in comforting contrast to the rough and chill grass around, which had dampened her skirts and shoes.

"I don't want to go any further, Angel," she said, stretching out her hand for his. "Can't we bide here?"

Thomas Hardy,
Tess of the d'Urbervilles, 1891

Henry Moore

For English sculptor Henry Moore (1898–1986), who visited Stonehenge regularly all his life, the site represents a source of esthetic and spiritual inspiration.

B elow, a sculpture by Henry Moore inspired by Stonehenge; on the following pages, a selection of his lithographs.

First visit to Stonehenge

Henry Moore describes his first visit to the site. He had recently arrived in London to study at the Royal College of Art.

Soon after settling into my digs, a tiny bedroom in Sydney Street, Chelsea, (it must have been towards the end of September or early October 1921) I decided one weekend to go and see Stonehenge. I took the train to

Salisbury arriving in the early evening, found a small hotel but by this time it was getting dark. After eating I decided I wouldn't wait to see Stonehenge until the next day.

As it was a clear evening I got to Stonehenge and saw it by moonlight. I was alone and tremendously impressed. (Moonlight, as you know, enlarges everything, and the mysterious depths and distances made it seem enormous.)

I went again the next morning, it was still very impressive, but that first moonlight visit remained for years my idea of Stonehenge.

In two or three lithographs I've tried to remember this moonlight effect. In those days, like many other things now spoiled by crowds, I don't remember anyone else being there, in the evening, or in the daytime.

Since that first visit to Stonehenge, I must have been there again twenty or

thirty times. Mary was for five years or more a boarder at Cranbourne Chase School, and twice every term we drove to Crichel. On these occasions we stayed the night in Salisbury, and many times we went to look at Stonehenge. Quite often I took photographs, and now and then made little sketches.

Perhaps a little point I may not have mentioned is that I began doing the album as etchings, and only later decided lithographs would be better. Etchings are done with a point making a fine line, the technique isn't a natural one for representing the texture of rough stone, whereas lithography is chalk on stone and more natural to get the texture of stone. Also, blackness is more natural to lithography, and the night, the moonlight idea was more possible.

Henry Moore,
from a letter to Stephen Spender,
in Henry Moore,
Stonehenge, 1974

Poet Stephen Spender analyzes the works of Henry Moore

The early lithographs are, for the most part, descriptive of the Stonehenge which the tourist knows. As with the etchings of the elephant's skull, the subject is easily recognizable because it is seen from a distance sufficient to include the whole of a trilithon arch, which its two sarsen pillars and its lintel placed above them; or the curved interiors of an oval of columns, a strange colonnade. However the "outside" scenes move from the

descriptive to the metaphorical. A long lintel resting on two columns conveys an almost elastic tension: the great reclining uplifted slab has immense weight. Yet it seems almost awake, poised there like a sarcophagus containing something sinister, a mummy or a body—ghostly. The incised narrower end of this horizontal form suggests the enclosed shoulders and head and neck of a corpse....

Thus a trilithon seen edge-on like head and limbs suggests to me the hunched body, arms and legs, forming almost a continuous line, and dog-nosed head of an Egyptian sculpture in the British Museum. Below this figure there lies a flat slab in what seems a pool of water, like a prostrate victim....

These monoliths, seen in the outside light, have the cruel power of the men who hauled them immense distances and who hammered and hacked at the stone developing its magical properties of power, intrinsic with the material itself.

Stephen Spender,
in Henry Moore,
Stonehenge, 1974

Stonehenge decoded

Gerald Hawkins addresses the function of Stonehenge, not as an archaeologist but as an astrophysicist using computer-assisted analysis. The results astonished the author himself: the correlation between computations and observations was unexpectedly close.

This Hawkins diagram of Stonehenge demonstrates the correlation between the architecture of the site and the positions of the sun and moon.

Does the arrangement of the standing stones at Stonehenge correspond to specific astronomical positions?

For Hawkins, too many parameters are in accord for there to be any doubt that Stonehenge is an instrument that could calculate the positions of the sun and of the moon 3,500 years ago.

We decided to try the most obvious celestial bodies, those prehistoric deities, the sun and the moon.

This time the result was astonishing. Repeatedly and closely those declinations which the machine had computed seemed to fit extreme positions of the sun—which I had suspected that they might—and also—which I had *not* suspected—the moon. Pair after pair of those significant Stonehenge positions seemed to point to the maximum declinations of the two most significant objects in the sky.

I say "seemed" because at that stage we were using a preliminary search program of no great celestial accuracy. The stone alignments and resulting declinations as produced by the machine were as exact as the original chart allowed, but we did not then have correspondingly precise positions for the sun and moon as of the time of Stonehenge. We were using rough approximations, gotten by mentally chasing those objects backward 4000 years in time. To verify the apparent correlations we needed precise sun-moon extreme positions as of 1500 BC.

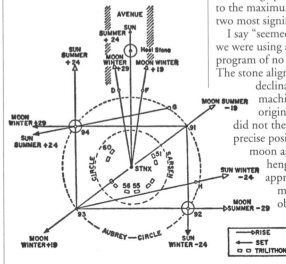

Back, of course, to the machine.

We gave it the present solar-lunar extreme declinations and the rate of change, and instructed it to determine what the extreme declinations had been in 1500 BC. At the same time we programmed the machine to calculate the direction of rise and set of the sun and moon. Not knowing what the Stonehengers might have chosen we allowed three definitions: (a) sun just showing, (b) sun's disk cut in half by horizon, and (c) disk standing tangent on the horizon. There is about 1° difference between the direction of (a) and (c) which of course is not very great, but I wanted to determine if possible what the Stonehengers had chosen as their definition.

And now I must try the reader's patience with some more basic astronomy. I must explain a little about the moon.

I have explained that the sun moves from a northernmost maximum position of +23.5° declination in summer to a corresponding −23.5° extreme southern declination in winter. Just the reverse motion is true of the full moon. It goes north in winter, south in summer. And it has a more complicated relative motion than the sun; it has two northern and two southern maxima. In an 18.61-year cycle it swings so that its far north and south declinations move from 29° to 19° and back to 29°. Thus it has two extremes, 29° and 19°, north and south. This pendulum-like relative motion is caused by the combined effects of tilt and precession of the orbit and it is much too difficult to clarify quickly; even an astronomer has trouble visualizing the processes involved. Here it is only necessary to understand that the moon *does* have two extreme positions for every one of the sun.

To position the sun and moon as of 1500 BC took the machine a few more seconds. The declinations it reported were ±23.9° for the sun and ±29.0° and ±18.7° for the moon. The most cursory glance showed us that those declinations were close, very close, to the ones determined by the Stonehenge alignments.

We compared the figures carefully. There was no doubt. Those important and often duplicated Stonehenge alignments were oriented to the sun and moon. And the orientation was all but complete.

As I have said, I was prepared for *some* Stonehenge–sun correlation. I was not prepared for total sun correlation—and I had not at all suspected that there might be almost total moon correlation as well. For what the machine's figures showed was this:

To a mean accuracy of less than one degree, 12 of the significant Stonehenge alignments pointed to an extreme position of the sun. And to a mean accuracy of about a degree and a half, 12 of the alignments pointed to an extreme of the moon....

Not one of the most significant Stonehenge positions failed to line up with another to point to some unique sun or moon position. Often the same Stonehenge position was paired with more than one other to make additional alignments. And of the 12 unique sun–moon rise–set points, only two— the midsummer moonsets at −29° and −19°—were not thus marked.

Gerald S. Hawkins,
Stonehenge Decoded,
1965

The Gavrinis images

*The discovery of megalithic art
was disconcerting to 19th-
century antiquarians. Prosper
Mérimée (1803–70), the first
Inspector of Historic Monuments in France, recognized
megalithic art as more than
mere ornamentation. But its
meaning eluded him.*

An engraved stone from the tumulus at Gavrinis.

"Bizarre drawings"

Besides its underground location, what
distinguishes the monument of
Gavrinis from all the dolmens I have
seen is that almost all the stones that
make up its walls are carved and
covered with bizarre drawings. These
are curves, straight lines, broken lines,
in a hundred different combinations.

The best comparison I can make is to
the tattoos of island dwellers of New
Zealand, whose heads are ornamented in
this way in Natural History Museum
exhibits. Often a single stone is divided
up into something akin to compartments that set off a portion of the
drawings from the background and
frame them. In carving all these
extraordinary lines, the artists did not
take the trouble first to clean the stone
surface, because nearly everywhere we
find those irregular undulations made by
a break in a block of granite; and yet
none of them offer excessive roughness.
The line of the images, engraved as a
hollow about a half-inch deep, forms
something like a trench, narrower at the
bottom than on the surface. Here and
there some images stand out in relief
against the background, like those of the
Table des Marchands at Locmariaquer.

Among a multitude of bizarre lines
that can only be considered ornaments, a
small number show a regularity and
unusual arrangement that resembles
written characters; they are very
elongated triangles, quite similar to
wedges, or else to those strange instruments of flint or jade known in common
parlance as Celts or celtic axes. In a
reserved space near the top of the fifth
stone of the southern wall (counting
from the west) we find eight of these
wedges arranged in three horizontal lines,

The interior of Gavrinis as depicted in the 19th century.

some with the point to the top, the others pointing downward. The fifth stone of the opposite wall has four in a single line. Still others are found on the fourth and fifth stones of the north wall, but no more than one or two each time. The wedges of the fourth stone (south wall) are unlike all the others: their points are opposite to one another. Often the base of these wedges is rounded, and sometimes closed off by two lines that meet at an extreme obtuse angle.

Cuneiform writing?

With just a bit of imagination we might consider these a series of inscriptions in cuneiform characters; however, in examining them carefully, we find only a small number of distinct combinations, which are moreover repeated so often that it is impossible to consider them as letters of an unknown written language. There are four of these combinations, defined by the horizontal or vertical positions of the wedge and of its point. It is clear on several stones, however, that two wedges have been brought together deliberately in such a way as to form a distinct group. If we count this joining of signs by twos, the number of combinations is raised to six; because we can distinguish two groups, one with the point upward, and the others reversed. We might even consider as a seventh combination the joining of two wedges placed vertically, one raised, the other pointing downward. Finally, it is possible to recognize an eighth character, if we accept as a particular sign a wedge with the point downward, above which a kind of oval is traced like a dot on an "i" (seventh stone of the south wall). It will be noted that a single combination is represented up to five times on the same stone (two wedges with the point downward). This small number of signs and their repetition seem to me to prove that they are not characters of any kind of written language. That the men who carved them must have associated them with some idea, a meaning, and that this is more than just an ornament, appears to me beyond any doubt; but as for the meaning, who today can hope to discover it?

Prosper Mérimée,
Notes on a Monument on the Isle of Gâvr'Innis, 1858

Megalithic art

Megalithic art includes pictures that are, to at least some degree, abstract, incised, sculpted, or painted on the slabs and blocks of monuments. These images first went unnoticed, then were judged incomprehensible—by Mérimée, for instance, speaking of Gavrinis. But increasingly, as research has advanced, megalithic art has come to be better understood.

A mother goddess.

Three major centers emerged initially: Brittany, western Iberia, and Ireland.

Breton art

Breton art is both homogeneous and copious. It is precocious and covers three millennia. The major themes seem to remain constant through the successive styles. This art is found on the columns of dolmens as well as on certain menhirs. It is produced primarily by chipping the rock, although there are examples of sculpture. The following styles can be distinguished:

The early sober style, characterized by pictures drawn with simple, often isolated lines. The motifs in Breton art—shield idol or "disheveled" idol, ax with or without handle, crook, U signs sometimes interpreted as bovine horns—are classic. These pictures are found on slabs of the oldest megalithic monuments of the 4th millennium BC. They occur as far away as Charente (France).

The monumental style seems to be reserved to the great menhirs of the Carnac region, and each motif measures several feet in size: idol, ax, plow-ax, crook, bull. Fragments of these giant monoliths were re-used to build dolmens around 4000 BC.

The "baroque" style echoes classic themes of the idol, the ax, and the crook, signs like the letters U or V, and repeats the lines in order to cover the surface of the slabs. The finest example is at Gavrinis, where the motifs of the bow and serpent have been added. It dates to the beginning of the 4th millennium BC.

The "plastic" style and associated styles at first concern the depiction of the female idol with breasts defined in a

Breton art

1. Cup mark, 2. U sign, 3. hornlike form, 4. crook, 5.–8. axes, 9. ax-plow, 10. shield idol, and 11. serpentine form.

round lump, found in the Breton gallery graves. The idol is decorated with concentric circles in the angled dolmen of Pierres Plates. In addition there are pictures of an ax and a "baton." This style and these motifs are also found in the Paris basin.

Western Iberian art

Western Iberian art is the field that can offer the greatest surprises, as attested to by the recent excavations of the monuments of Soto (Helva), Navalcan (Toledo), and Alberite (Cadiz), dating from the 5th millennium. Paintings and chipped designs are often complementary, as for instance on this "statue-menhir" painted red and with chipped-out serpents, which was found at the entrance to the dolmen of Navalcan.... One exception is a painted scene representing a man with bow aiming at deer at the dolmen of Juncaïs at Viseu, Portugal.

The "realist" tendency also includes a handled goblet typical of the Portuguese dolmens. The sun and moon are chipped out on the standing

Western Iberian art

1. Anthropomorph and handled goblet, 2. animal design, 3.–4. floral motif, 5.–6. serpentine forms, 7.–8. sun, and 9. U signs.

stones as well as on the painted slabs of dolmens.

Geometric motifs, large zigzags, floral motifs, or simple cup marks seem to decorate entire surfaces at Soto or Alberite, prompting archaeologists to comment that these chambers were true temple sanctuaries before their entrance was sealed off.

Irish art

Irish art is rather late (late 4th millennium BC) and very homogeneous. It is characterized by circular motifs or spirals and lozenges or zigzags. Two styles have been distinguished depending on the style in which the motifs were depicted. The orderly style is represented by the blocks at Newgrange, Ireland, while the free style is found at Loughcrew.

Some slabs show a composition resembling a body surmounted by two eyes; it is assumed to be anthropomorphic and represents the guardian divinity of the sanctuary tombs.

"Mother goddess" and statue-menhir

The three anthropomorphic monoliths at the entrance of the three chambers of cairn III at Gennog (Finistère,

Brittany), the steles with the "shield" profile like that of the Table des Marchands, and the shield idol chipped out on several slabs, presenting characteristics shared by the steles, seem all to express the same theme. In fact, when this personage is treated in a more realistic manner, in the steles of Kermené, Le Trévoux, and Le Catel, or on the slabs of gallery graves of Brittany or the Paris basin, the pronounced breasts, along with the necklace, symbolize femininity. Throughout the Neolithic era, this character Jacques Cauvin called the "mother goddess" in reference to the divinity of the pro-oriental Neolithic age, in fact would be omnipresent in the megalithic monuments.

Not until the following period, beginning with the Chalcolithic, were the statue-menhirs of southern France, Switzerland, and Italy divided between female and male. The arms of the males were represented.

Jean-Pierre Mohen

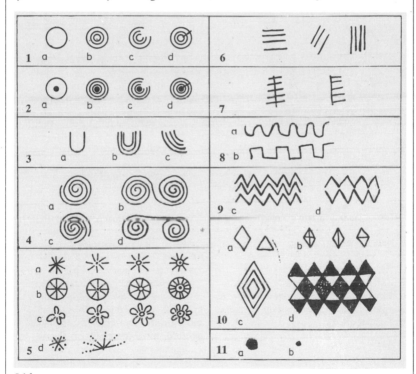

Irish art

1.–2. Circular motifs, 3. U signs, 4. spirals, 5. sun and star, 6.–7. rectilinear motifs, 9. angled motifs, and 10. lozenges.

Hauling a megalith: a command performance

To attempt to move a megalith today in the way it was done 3,000 to 6,000 years ago requires more than a massive input of technical know-how. There is nothing simple about this sort of experiment.

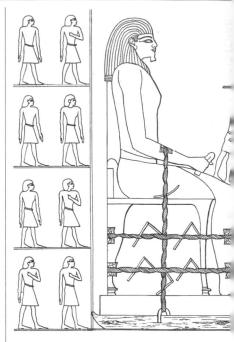

The contribution of ancient images

Ancient iconography provides us with a few images that have become classic, including the famous Egyptian depiction of the tomb of Djehuty Hetep at El Bershi. The relief shows the hauling of a colossal statue estimated at 60 tons, which was secured on a sledge drawn by four rows of haulers attached by rope. Standing on the knees of the colossus is the foreman who directs the job, and, facing him, we see a figure who is probably a priest.

Another relief, an Assyrian work in the British Museum, also shows us the hauling of a monumental sculpture with the aid of runners and a crowd that provided the manpower necessary for such an operation.

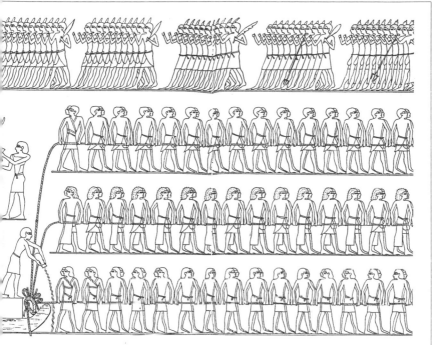

There are certain points shared by these illustrations and tales told by travelers to Madagascar, India, or Indonesia in the past century, or even in the early years of our own: the handling of the great stones demands a powerful massing of population, and the collective project gave rise to a scene of festivity. There is a direct relationship between the weight of the block and the human energy mobilized. This balance between the inert material mass and the movement implied by the gathering of all these human lives appears essential in the process of constructing the temple in honor of the god or building the tomb in homage to the pharaoh or an illustrious ancestor.

From this evidence, the installation of a megalith, since it is the nature of a

Moving a colossal statue in ancient Egypt, from a depiction in a tomb.

megalith to be particularly heavy, implies the participation of a great number of people. In assuming this effort and this challenge, they experience a certain euphoria sustained to varying degrees by drink, as well as by religious, ethnic, or clannish motives.... In Madagascar, the overflowing of vital energy in the successful completion of the funerary rite of the Malagasy dolmens becomes the motivating event of the society.

Excavations of the Bougon necropolis revealed the tools used by the Neolithic quarrymen; they were found deep within quarries bordering each tumulus. These tools were antler picks and flint hammers for cutting up blocks of stone of more than 100 pounds which would form the tumulus and its curbing. The same tools must have been used on the sides of plateaus that were rich in the great slabs, not far from the necropolis. But these tools were not sufficient. To undertake this reconstruction, we had to make use of wooden levers, rollers, and gliders or rails that could be disassembled. It was also necessary to imagine the ropes such as those that are a regular feature of lakeside excavations in the regions of the Alps and the Jura. We had to prepare nearly 450 pounds of flax rope to wrap like a net around the 32-ton block and to connect it to the six rows of haulers.

Bougon, 28 July 1979

It was the morning of 28 July 1979, and nearly 900 people had assembled, either to help haul the block or to watch. Those who were there to work were divided into small teams and each leader explained the role each would play. Five independent teams of six to eight persons practiced manipulating the oak rollers and rails, each of which weighed more than 600 pounds, and set them in place in front of the block while another team was put to work raising the ropes with long poles. On the first attempt at hauling, the ropes were pulled taut, but a roller seemed to be stuck, and the block did not move forward. A lever had to be used to remove the immobilized roller and replace it. On the second attempt, 230 men pulled and 20 pushed, the ropes became taut once again, and the block started to move, carried by its weight amid a great clatter of rollers. A distance of almost 20 feet [6 meters] was covered. From the uproar, you would have thought a major event had taken place.

In this way, the block was hauled in

several stages over the course of the morning, as the removable path, with its rails and rollers, would be retrieved from behind the block and placed in front. About 130 feet [40 meters] were covered. One stage of hauling was accomplished with 170 men pulling and 20 dislodging the block from behind with small individual levers. At first the work was done with the rope held at shoulder level and with some men advancing. In some experiments, the men walked backward holding the rope at waist level, which

Hauling a megalith at Bougon, Deux-Sèvres, France.

seemed to be even more effective.

Just one difficulty emerged from this experiment: Despite the precautions taken during its transport to maintain the block straight in the axis of the removable path, and no doubt because of the irregularity of one of the rollers, the block started to veer off during the second and third stage of hauling. A great lever, 33 feet long [10 meters], handled by some 20 men, was placed exactly at the spot indicated by J. Bezombes, Jr., and it was thus possible to steer the block back into the axis of the removable path, and the experiment was able to continue.

The principle of the great lever was

applied on the afternoon of 28 July 1979 to raise the 32-ton block without the aid of a ramp. It was sufficient to place three large levers on one of the short ends of the block, to depress their ends at the same time in order to raise it. The void thus created was filled by a crosspiece of wood that maintained the block at its new height. Once removed, the levers were placed on the other side. Thus, by a play of levers and a system of interlocking beams, the block was raised to the desired height. During this experiment it was raised by about 3 feet.

Jean-Pierre Mohen,
Les Dossiers de l'archéologie,
September–October 1980

Bougon, 22 June 1997

The hauling experiment was repeated at Bougon on 25 June 1995 with the same block and the same system of ropes and logs. Improvement in the technique led to a reduction of the number of haulers to 120—quite a striking result.

The following year, an advertisement appeared in newspapers announcing that on Sunday, 22 June 1997, "We shall attempt to move [the 32-ton slab] with fewer than fifty persons, without either pulling or pushing and without ropes." Bernard Poissonnier, an archaeologist with the Centre d'Etudes des techniques et de recherches expérimentales en préhistoire (Belgium), came with his friends to test a pet theory of his: "We made holes in some wooden logs at several points, which enabled them to be turned on themselves with the help of various levers. That made the stone move." These logs were in fact rollers

that propelled the stone forward: they became hubs and the levers became the spokes of a "proto-wheel." With this system we'll call rotative, effort is concentrated and the number of participants becomes minimal. In fact, only some ten people are needed to move the block.

The new experiment depends on a clever technique that shows that technology alone was certainly not a major handicap for the builders of megaliths. This system has never been reported, and for the moment it seems to be a modern invention. We saw that the problem was not to reduce radically the number of participants in this great festival that was the installation of a huge stone. A more traditional technique was perhaps more in keeping with the spirit of this gigantic operation. It is impressive indeed to compare the 32 tons of the Bougon experiment with the 350 tons of the Great Broken Menhir of Locmariaquer, a weight that probably required the invention of techniques as elaborate as Bernard Poissonnier's.

Jean-Pierre Mohen

Glossary

Alignment Series of standing stones in a straight line. There can be several parallel rows, as at Carnac in Brittany. An alignment is sometimes accompanied by an oval or rectangular enclosure also set off by standing stones.

Alignments.

Antechamber Front portion of a megalithic tomb or hypogeum, separate from the chamber but of the same size. This sets it apart from the portico and passage.

Anthropomorphic Shaped like a human silhouette, like some sculpted stone slabs found in Brittany that have shoulder indications and evoke the shield idol.

Anthropomorphic slab Monolith of considerable height (above 3 feet, or 1 meter) with a facial likeness and a few attributes carved in low relief on one side, or more simply with a human silhouette consisting of shoulders and a peak suggesting the head.

Avenue Long alley lined with ditches and earthen banks leading to a ceremonial central area. Stonehenge is an example.

Burial, or inhumation This term applies, in the widest sense, to any custom of depositing a corpse or human bones, even when they are not covered by earth. It is thus distinguished from cremation.

Burial chamber Construction of stone or wood measuring more than 6 by 3 feet, or 2 by 1 meters, on the outside and 3 feet (1 meter) high inside, and is thus distinguished from the coffer and the cist. The chamber usually contains collective tombs.

Cairn Tumulus or mound of a megalithic tomb made up of small stones.

Cave Burial site where the remains of the departed are kept.

Cella Closed sacred space in a temple or burial chamber.

Chamber tomb Closed burial space situated underground or inside a tumulus, and with interior dimensions greater than those of a cist or coffer, that is more than 6 feet long, 3 feet wide, and 3 feet high (or 2 by 1 by 1 meters). The chamber tomb is usually a collective tomb. It is approached by various means that are not always easy to recognize: by moving aside a stone slab or by clearing away loose stones, for example.

Circle General term designating any circular structure, mainly a circle of standing stones, sometimes surrounded by a ditch, a raised mound, or a fence.

Cist By analogy with the Latin *cista* meaning "small basket with cover," this term refers to a small construction made of drystone or with vertical and horizontal stone slabs. A cist shelters an individual tomb, which distinguishes it from the coffer.

Coffer Burial construction of stone or wood of modest dimensions, usually entered from above. Generally it does not exceed 6 by 3 feet in size and 3 feet in interior height (2 by 1 by 1 meters), which distinguishes it from the burial chamber. A coffer is intended to hold collective tombs, unlike the cist.

Column/pillar Block or slab supporting the covering stone of a megalithic chamber or its passage.

Corbeling "So-called oven vault, formed by successively stacking [cantilevered] stones until they meet or until a slab is used as keystone" (Jean Arnal, 1956).

Court-cairn Tumulus with a forecourt. In Ireland the court can be internal, with the mound completely surrounding it. An external court is simply set off by a concave facade.

Cremation This funerary practice, often difficult to recognize, was more widespread than originally believed. Common in Ireland, cremation seems to have appeared sporadically in the megalithic tombs of other regions.

Cromlech Welsh term for a stone slab supported by blocks; it is equivalent to a dolmen. Also, more generally, it is the circle formed by blocks surrounding a mound that covers a megalithic chamber; these stones form a peristyle. By extension, some authors have used this term to denote any megalithic circle or enclosure.

Crook Megalithic art motif seen in Breton tombs and on statues or menhirs in southern France. Its profile recalls the votive crooks of engraved schist found in Portuguese megalithic tombs as well as a wooden club found at Auvernier-Saunerie on the banks of Lake Neuchâtel (Switzerland).

Culture Archaeological term for a homogeneous set of material evidence (tools, arms, jewelry, residences, funerary rites, and so on) of which the traces can be observed. Culture has geographic and chronological limits. Within a single culture, various features (pottery or architecture, for example) can be distinguished. Several cultures can form a civilization, such as the Neolithic civilization of Western Europe, Greek civilization, or Roman civilization.

Cupmark Small hollow made in a slab or rock. Often grouped together, these indentations result from a repeated ritual gesture, the significance of which is unclear.

Curb Piled-up stones forming a wall to limit and retain the various elements of a tumulus.

Cromlech.

Dolmen Welsh for "stone table," the most common remnant from the burial chamber of a megalithic monument. "Although the place name Tolmaen is found on a plan or monastery record in Landevennec for an undetermined place, it was Théophile de La Tour d'Auvergne who popularized the barbarism *dolmin* used by Legrand d'Aussi and *dolmen,* used by J. Cambry (instead of *taolven,* the correct term for a stone table). Through flexible usage, the term has no value now except as a very general term for any megalithic sculpture" (Pierre-Roland Giot, 1979). According to Jean Arnal in

Dolmen.

1956, "The dolmen is an open burial chamber, generally megalithic, covered with a tumulus and used to hold several burials."

Drystone Building style using stone slabs piled on top of one another without any bonding material such as clay or mortar to form walls and curbs.

Funeral rites Series of ceremonies that determine the attitude of the living toward their dead. A distinction is made between primary rites, such as the ossuary or cave ritual, and secondary rites, such as reliquary ritual.

Gallery grave (or long stone cist) Its significance varies considerably, as does the form it takes, depending on the author consulted. The only constant seems to be the extreme length of the chamber passage, which is lined with stone slabs. Among the main types of gallery grave are:

- the Armorican type, built above ground and covered with a series of stone slabs under a long tumulus. It consists of an antechamber and a terminal cell, which is sometimes decorated. The buttressed gallery grave uses lateral stone slabs leaning toward the center, propping each other up.

- the Aquitainian type, built above ground, distinguished by the increasing height of the lateral pillars in the direction of the headstone.

- the Aude type, with antechamber and chamber that decrease in height.

- the Paris basin type, situated in a trench with a sometimes decorated antechamber. Walls in this type of gallery grave can be of drystone or wood. Frequently the covering seems not to be megalithic. These monuments and the hypogea of the Marne are linked by iconography and ritual.

G allery grave.

- the gallery grave from Westphalia or Hesse, Germany, also known as Steinkiste, with axial entry. Some of these monuments have a lateral entry, as for instance in a series of tombs in Denmark, northern Germany, Holland, and Brittany, which are not referred to as gallery graves.

Giants' grave In Sardinia, a very long megalithic tomb covered with blocks, with wings on either side and a concave facade; the monumental front consists of a large sculpted slab over a low entryway.

Giant tumulus These mounds, circular or elongated, are marked by vast dimensions (more than 325 feet, or 100 meters, in length or diameter, and more than 13 feet, or 4 meters, high), discreet funerary references (though not in all cases), obvious links to megalithic monuments (curbs, orientation, shape of graves, and similar dates of construction).

Grave goods Grave goods consist of offerings left in the tomb or nearby.

Headstone Wall slab opposite the entrance of a megalithic chamber. The finest example of a headstone (or apsidal stone) is in the tomb of the Table des Marchands at Locmariaquer (Brittany) with its anthropomorphic profile and its crook decoration.

Henge English term traditionally used for a circular structure. It can consist of a ditch, usually accompanied with an earthen mound and/or a series of standing stones. The variety of elements in this open architecture can be observed at Stonehenge; see Circle.

Hougue, or hogue Mound, in Norman (northern French) dialect.

Hypogeum This specific type of rock-cut tomb consists of a burial chamber preceded by a smaller antechamber, which is approached from outside through a sloping passage.

Idol Anthropomorphic representation, either an often-stylized statuette of terra-cotta, bone, or stone, or an image chipped out on slabs of megalithic tombs. One of these figures, called a shield or "disheveled" idol, is highly abstract in form.

Megalith; megalithic Block of stone of large dimensions (from Greek *mega*=large, and *lithos*= stone), installed and incorporated into an architecture called megalithic. Megalithic architecture is simple when it involves a standing stone in an intentional relationship with the natural elements of a landscape. It is open but more complex if several standing stones are aligned or arranged in a circle; Stonehenge provides the most striking example of this type. It is closed when the blocks are used to construct a temple cell (temples of the Maltese archipelago) or a burial chamber (tombs of the Maltese Atlantic region). In this last case, the megaliths are often associated with drystone curbs, earth, or rubble, or even with wooden structures; and the tombs are covered with a mound or tumulus.

Megalithism Worldwide phenomenon that consists of using large blocks of stone (megaliths), usually rough-cut. Megalithism is, in particular, one of the major characteristics of the western European Neolithic age. It appeared there from the 5th millennium BC in its monumental aspects and represents one of the earliest known stone architectures in the world. It is the major social and religious expression of human groups who acquired the agricultural way of life and became sedentary. Other countries on all continents have also known megalithism in specific chronological and anthropological contexts. These have been demonstrated, for instance, through the oral traditions of Malagasy society of the 18th and 19th centuries or even observed in Borneo around 1900. The study of megalithism is comparative, relying on original observations and convergent features.

Menhir The term (in the form of *minhir*, "long stone") became common among devotees of Celtic practices at the end of the 18th century. There is no proof that it is of popular origin, although it is found in many localities (in names such as Kermenhir). In his dictionary published in 1732, Dom Grégoire de Rostrenen gives the term *peulvan*—which refers to a standing stone—as a synonym for *menhir*.

Monolith; monolithic From the Greek *monos* (=sole) and *lithos* (=stone). A standing stone is a monolith. The monolithic covering for a chamber consists of a single stone slab.

Mortuary house (or house of the dead) Found in Denmark, a small structure of wood, mud, and straw in which the deceased was placed, along with offerings. It can contain several individuals; this sanctuary can serve as the basis for the construction of a large tumulus. This type of construction has been found elsewhere, such as in the British Isles.

Mound The funerary mound is the same thing as the tumulus.

Naveta On the island of Minorca, a long burial chamber covered with blocks.

Necropolis From the Greek *necros* (=dead) and *polis* (=city), the word means "city of the dead" and implies two notions, one concerning architecture and the other the funerary function. The necropolis is distinguished from the cemetery by its architecture; it can become a sanctuary when its funerary function is sublimated.

Nuraghe In Sardinia, a tower built in a cyclopean style.

Offering Any object left as a gift to an ancestor or semi-divinity. Offerings are found in a tomb or at the base of a standing stone. While it can be individual, an offering seems in general to be collective.

Orthostat Standing stone slab that forms the wall of a megalithic tomb or an element of such a wall.

Ossuary Burial site where corpses are piled up following some carnage, an epidemic, or a natural death.

Passage "A corridor not as wide or high as the burial chamber and leading to the chamber from the periphery of the mound" (Jean Arnal, 1956).

Menhir.

Passage grave Burial chamber with entry passage leading to the funerary center of the monument from the outer edge of the tumulus. The passage grave is often all that remains of a tomb once the tumulus has been eroded.

Peulvan Ancient Breton name for a standing stone in the area around Audierne.

Pit Usually a hole dug in the ground, most often filled in. There are foundation pits, the well-known "post holes," and holes that had held the base of columns, wall slabs, or standing stones. Wedging stones are often found in pits. The foundation pit sometimes contains an offering that sanctifies the monument, such as with certain standing stones. There are also burial pits containing cremated or exhumed remains; such remains can be either single or collective.

Portal dolmen In Ireland or Wales, a kind of megalithic chamber resembling, in its ruined phase, a great portico with an enormous covering stone supported on two columns.

Porthole slab Perforated slab found at the entry to some burial chambers.

Portico Megalithic trilithon (structure made of two upright stones and a horizontal lintel) placed at the entry of certain tombs, such as those of the Anjou type.

Reliquary Place for storing a relic, which might be all or part of a skeleton or an embalmed corpse considered sacred.

Re-use Megalithic tombs often show several successive phases of use, indicated by particular arrangements of bones, by connected structures of small slabs, or by grave goods from various cultures. Re-use can sometimes involve continuity of the initial rite, using the same entry and the same arrangements (body placed in a crouching position, for instance). In such examples, earlier skeletons might be rearranged to make more space; their bones might be placed along the sides of the chamber. At times re-use can occur considerably later than the first use of the grave—a thousand years or more—following rites different from the earlier ones.

Rock-cut tomb or artificial cave Underground monument hollowed out of solid rock and usually intended to hold a collective grave. Artificial grottoes are frequent in the Mediterranean basin. This general term also refers to a specific type with an antechamber, called a hypogeum. It makes sense to associate artificial grottoes closely with megalithic monuments, as the two have several points of chronology, function, and iconography in common.

Sanctuary A constructed site for the practice of ceremonial rites according to religious and spiritual values. A necropolis can become a sanctuary when the burial function has ceased. A sanctuary can exist without any association with burial, but this is a rare situation because any metaphysical dimension tends to begin with death.

Sealing off Once a megalithic tomb has received its funerary deposits and its offerings, it is often sealed off: first, the access passage is blocked by loose stones and hidden by a curb or by a stone slab; then the monument, especially the facade, is covered by a pile of loose stones. Sometimes it seems that certain wooden or stone structures have been voluntarily destroyed, by fire for instance. Although it was sealed off after its first use, the monument could still be venerated, as later re-uses prove.

Shield A carved or incised design found on the slabs of Breton tombs depicting an anthropomorphic face in very abstract terms. Shields were apparently intended to be idols.

Slab Large flat stone that is usually not very thick. Smaller slabs can be used for paving or partitions.

Standing, or raised, stone Any stone used by human beings to mark a place, a recollection, an homage, or a veneration. Also referred to as a menhir or peulvan.

Statue-menhir Monolith depicting "the human body in its totality, on the front and rear surfaces, sculpted in low relief or sometimes engraved. They vary from 75 centimeters to 4 meters in height. In form they are generally rectangular or subrect-angular, but the top may be rounded or pointed" (André d'Anna, 1977).

Stele Modest-size monolith with only one side decorated with cut-away carvings or sculpture in low relief.

Table The single covering stone of the megalithic tomb in the traditional concept of the "dolmen."

Talayot Cyclopean-style tower containing one or more chambers, on the island of Minorca.

Taula In Minorca, a massive column with a block balanced on its top and standing in a circular area surrounded by a stone wall.

Temple Megalithic temples of the islands of Malta,

Gozo, and Sardinia are buildings with vast internal space, not necessarily funerary.

Tholos Term used erroneously in referring to Mycenean tombs, to designate circular vaulted chambers with passage entrance.

Tomb From Latin *tumba*, meaning a burial stone, simple or monumental. In a very general sense, tombs refer to megalithic graves.

Torre A cyclopean-style tower found in southern Corsica, the equivalent of the talayot of the Balearic Islands.

Transept Occasionally a megalithic passage grave can have two, and sometimes four, lateral compartments, which form a transept (crossing) or double transept.

Tumulus Latin term for an artificial mound covering a burial deposit; it can range from a simple pile of burned bones to a megalithic tomb, which is therefore known as a megalithic tumulus. Externally it seldom resembles a simple earthen mound (a tumulus in the strict sense) or pile of stones (a cairn). It is often surrounded by a series of blocks or a drystone curb and can even have a supplementary wooden structure; a facade is sometimes built at the entry to the grave.

Unchambered barrow Tumulus without a burial chamber. It can be either elongated or circular, and it usually presents some reference to burial (such as a simple pile of bones).

Adapted from Jean-Pierre Mohen,
Le Monde des mégalithes
(The World of the Megaliths), Paris, 1989

Further Reading

GENERAL

Clarke, David V., T. G. Cowie, and Andrew Foxon, *Symbols of Power at the Time of Stonehenge*, 1985

Masset, Claude, *Les Dolmens: Sociétés néolithiques et pratiques funéraires : les sépultures collectives d'Europe occidentale*, 1993

Mohen, Jean-Pierre, *The World of Megaliths*, Helen McPhail (trans.), 1990

Piggott, Stuart, *Neolithic Cultures of the British Isles*, 1954

CONSTRUCTION, SCIENCE, ART

Cauvin, Jacques, *Naissance des divinités, Naissance de l'agriculture, La révolution des symboles au Néolithique*, 1994

Coles, John, *Experimental Archeology*, 1979

d'Anna, André, *Les Statues-menhirs et stèles anthropomorphes du Midi de la France*, 1977

Devignes, Marc (ed.), "L'art des mégalithes peints et gravés, France, Espagne, Portugal, Irlande, Grande-Bretagne," *Dossiers de l'Archéologie*, no. 230

Hawkins, Gerald. S., *Stonehenge Decoded*, 1965

Heggie, Douglas C., *Megalithic Science, Ancient Mathematics and Astronomy in Northwest Europe*, 1981

L'Helgouac'h, Jean, Charles-Tanguy LeRoux, Joël Lecornec (eds.), "Art et symboles du Mégalithisme européen," suppl. 8, *Revue Archéologique de l'Ouest*, 1996

Shee Twohig, Elizabeth, *The Megalithic Art of Western Europe*, 1981

Thom, Alexander, *Megalithic Remains in Britain and Brittany*, 1978

MEGALITHS IN EUROPE

Briard, Jacques, *Les Mégalithes de l'Europe*, 1995

Daniel, Glyn, *The Megalith Builders of Western Europe*, 1958

Daniel, Glyn, and Paul Kyaeram, *Megalithic Graves and Rituals*, 1973

Guilaine, Jean, *La Mer partagée, la Méditerrannée avant l'écriture, 7000–2000 av. J.-C.*

Hayman, Richard, *Riddles in Stone: Myths, Archaeology and the Ancient Britons*, 1997

Herity, Michael, *Irish Passage Graves*, 1974

Michell, John, *Megalithomania: Artists, Antiquarians and Archaeologists at the Old Stone Monuments*, 1982

Patton, Mark, *Statements in Stone: Monuments and Society in Neolithic Brittany*, 1993

Renfrew, Colin (ed.), *The Megalithic Monuments of Western Europe: The Latest Evidence Presented by Nine Leading Authorities*, 1983

MEGALITHS BEYOND EUROPE

Byung-mo Kim, *Megalithic Cultures in Asia*, 1982

Camps, Gabriel, *Aux origines de la Berbérie. Monuments et rites funéraires protohistoriques*, 1962

Chauvet, Stephen, *L'Ile de Pâques et ses mystères*, 1935

Fergusson, James, *Rude Stone Monuments in All Countries Throughout the World*, 1872

Joussaume, Roger, *Dolmens for the Dead: Megalith-Building Throughout the World*, trans. Anne and Christopher Chippindale, 1988

Mohen, Jean-Pierre, *Les Rites de l'au-delà*, 1995

Thilmans, G., Descamps, C., Khayat, B., *Protohistoire du Sénégal*, vol. 2: *Les Sites mégalithiques*, 1980

MONOGRAPHS ON THE MAJOR SITES DISCUSSED

Atkinson, Richard, *Stonehenge*, 1979

Burgess, Colin, *The Art of Stonehenge*, 1980

Burl, Aubrey, *Prehistoric Avebury*, 1979

Chippindale, Christopher, *Stonehenge Complete*, 1994

Eogan, George, *Excavations at Knowth*, 1984

———, *Knowth and the Passage-Tombs of Ireland*, 1981

O'Kelly, Michael J., "Newgrange," *Archaeology, Art and Legend*, 1982

Renfrew, Colin, *Investigations in Orkney*, 1979

List of Illustrations

Amenhir near Lochrist, France.

Cromlech from the Orkneys.

Index

Photograph Credits

AKG, Paris 114–15. All rights reserved 15a, 31, 33l, 33r, 34–35, 36, 37, 38–39, 40–41, 44–45, 45, 52, 64–65, 70, 74l, 74r, 75bl, 78r, 78b, 79a, 79b, 85a, 85b, 89, 90–91, 93, 96a, 106, 106–107, 107, 116–17, 122b, 127, 130, 131l, 131r, 134, 142, 143a, 143b, 148, 153, 154, 155, 160, 161, 163, 164, 167. Archives Gallimard Jeunesse 44, 48, 49, 132, 137, 151. Atkinson 121b, 125. Gérard Bailloud 35r, 139. Bibliothèque nationale, Paris 43. P. Birocheau/J.-M. Large 84–85. Bodleian Library, Oxford 24l, 24r, 24–25, 25a, 25b, 25c. Jean-Loup Charmet, Paris spine, 11, 12, 13, 14–15, 15b, 16, 17, 18–19, 19l, 20–21, 23a, 23b, 30, 46a, 46b, 47, 82b, 84b, 136. Collection Londres/R. J. Davis 29. Collection Londres/Fay Godwin 1–9, 116. Editions d'art Jos le Doaré, Chateaulin 56bn, 56–57, 57, 58a. Explorer 52–53. Explorer/S. Boiffin Vivier 105. Explorer/C. Cuny 80. Explorer/A. Froissardey 92–93. Explorer/Le Coz 65. Explorer/D. Mar 73. Explorer/Migdale 124. Explorer/G. Renoux 105b. Explorer/P. Roy 60b, 87. Explorer/ P. Tetrel 50. Explorer/H. Veiller 60–61. Gallimard/Vincent Lever 54a, 58c, 59bl, 59br, 60a, 60c, 62, 72, 72–73. J. Paul Getty Museum, Los Angeles 112–13. Jean-Claude Golvin 122a, 122–23. G. Hersant 96b, 98, 99a. Hoaqui/G. Gasquet 88–89. Hoaqui/C. Vaisse 70–71, 71bl. R. Joussaume 58b. Ian Kinnes 51, 53. J.-M. Labat 63a, 94, 95a, 94–95, 97a, 99b, 119, 152. G. Loison 82a. Magnum/Erich Lessing back cover, 66, 76, 103. Mairie de Meudon, Service des Archives 138. Masset 100–101, 101. Jean-Pierre Mohen 21, 54b, 55, 95b, 118, 120–21, 121a, 126–27, 126, 158, 159. Henry Moore Foundation 144, 144–45, 146, 147. National Museum of Dublin 97b. Office of Public Works, Dublin 59a, 77. Photo Researchers/Lawrence Mogdale 104a. Photograph Tarrotte 61b. Pierre Pitrou 28a, 28b, 34a, 34c, 34b, 42, 42–43a, 42–43c. R. Pollès 68a, 68b, 69. Salisbury and South Wiltshire Museum 26–27, 110–11. Sauzade 81. Scope/Charles Bowman front cover, 102, 124–25, 128. Scope/Jacques Gaillard 75r, 140–41. Scope/Michel Plassart 150. Märta Strömberg 83. Tarrette 61b. Victoria and Albert Museum, London 108–109. Viollet, Paris 16–17, 18, 19r, 22–23, 67a, 67b, 71b. Wiltshire Archaeological and Natural History Society, Devizes 32–33, 32, 33b.

Text Credits

From *Stonehenge Decoded* by Gerald S. Hawkins and John B. White. Copyright © 1965 by Gerald S. Hawkins and John B. White. Used by permission of Doubleday, a division of Random House, Inc., New York. From *Stonehenge* by Henry Moore, Ganymed Original Editions Ltd., London, 1974. By permission of The Henry Moore Foundation, Reprinted by permission of The Peters Fraser and Dunlop Group Limited on behalf of Stephen Spender: 1974 Introduction copyright Stephen Spender and Ganymed Original Editions Ltd.

Jean-Pierre Mohen received his doctorate in prehistory
at the Sorbonne, Paris, supervised by André Leroi-Gourhan.
He has curated numerous exhibitions at the Grand Palais in
Paris (Scythian Gold, 1975; Treasures of the Celtic Princes,
1987; The Vikings, 1992) and was the commissioner of
the French Year of Archaeology in 1989–90. His published
works include *The World of the Megaliths* (1990),
La Métallurgie préhistorique (1990), and *Les Rites de l'au-delà*
(1995). Mohen was director of the museum of St.-Germain-
en-Laye, France, from 1987 to 1992, and since 1992
he has served as director of the research laboratory of
the French National Museums.

Translated from the French by Dorie B. and David J. Baker

For Harry N. Abrams, Inc.
Editor: Sharon AvRutick
Typographic designers: Elissa Ichiyasu, Tina Thompson
Cover designer: Dana Sloan
Text permissions: Barbara Lyons

Library of Congress Cataloging-in-Publication Data

Mohen, Jean-Pierre, 1944–
    [Mégalithes. English]
    Megaliths : stones of memory / Jean-Pierre Mohen.
       p.   cm. — (Discoveries)
    Includes bibliographical references and index.
    ISBN 0-8109-2861-2 (pbk.)
    1. Megalithic monuments. I. Title. II. Series : Discoveries (New York, N.Y.)
GN790.M7313 1999
930.1'4—dc21   98–50716